From Your Friends At **The MAILBOX®** Magazine

AUGUST

A MONTH OF IDEAS AT YOUR FINGERTIPS!

PRESCHOOL– KINDERGARTEN

WRITTEN BY
Barbara Backer, Linda Blassingame, Stacie Davis,
Jayne Gammons, Linda Gordetsky, Ada Goren, Lucia Kemp Henry,
Lori Kent, Suzanne Moore, Vicki Mockaitis Pacchetti,
Mackie Rhodes, Dayle Timmons, Christina McElhoes Yuhouse

EDITED BY
Lynn Bemer Coble, Ada Goren, Mackie Rhodes, Laurel Robinson,
Jennifer Rudisill, Debbie Shoffner, Gina Sutphin

ILLUSTRATED BY
Pam Crane, Clevell Harris, Susan Hodnett, Sheila Krill,
Rob Mayworth, Kimberly Richard, Rebecca Saunders

TYPESET BY
Scott Lyons, Lynette Maxwell

COVER DESIGNED BY
Jennifer Bennett

©1997 by THE EDUCATION CENTER, INC.
All rights reserved except as here noted.
ISBN #1-56234-191-X

Manufactured in the United States

10 9 8 7 6 5 4 3 2 1

TABLE OF CONTENTS

August Calendar

Children's Vision And Learning Month

This monthlong campaign encourages parents to have an eye-care professional examine their children's eyes before the start of school. Reinforce the importance of eye care by reading aloud *Arthur's Eyes* by Marc Brown (Little, Brown & Company). Then have youngsters decorate an eyeglasses cutout with a variety of craft materials. Attach a parent note to each cutout explaining the importance of the Children's Vision campaign. Then have little ones take the reminders home.

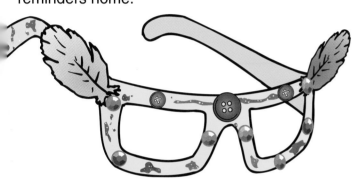

International Clown Week
(Annually, August 1–7)

Who doesn't love a clown? Celebrate the wholesome entertainment clowns provide by having a Clown Day at school. Invite students to dress up like clowns. Provide mirrors and a variety of face paints, and encourage youngsters to paint designs on their faces (or have adult or older child volunteers paint faces). Then lead your little tricksters on a parade around the school grounds. End this special day with a super circus snack of peanuts and popcorn. Hip, hip, hooray!

National Smile Week
(First Full Week In August)

"Share a smile and it will come back to you." Encourage your little ones to share their smiles this week. Snap a photo of each child doing something that makes him smile. Mount each photo on a separate sheet of construction paper. Ask each student to dictate something that makes him smile as you write his response under his picture. Compile the pages into a take-home book that families can read together—a surefire way to share some smiles!

Reading a book makes me smile.

Rosa

National Aviation Week
(Annually, The Week Of August 19)

This annual event is held each year during the week of Orville Wright's birthday (August 19). Take a class poll to see how many of your students have flown in an airplane or other mode of air transportation. Then challenge small groups of students to work cooperatively to build their own flying machines using collage materials such as paper-towel tubes, tagboard, construction paper, pipe cleaners, and glue. Up, up and away!

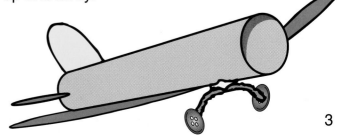

Friendship Day
(First Sunday In August)

Oh, you've got to have friends! Focus on friendships by singing "Friends Forever" by Greg & Steve on *We All Live Together: Vol. 5* (Youngheart Music, Inc.). After singing the song, invite each student to make a card to give to a special friend in appreciation of his friendship.

9—Book Lovers Day

Give a book to your class on this special day. Wrap a new book in wrapping paper; then tie it up with a big bow and leave it in a prominent place in your classroom. Encourage students to guess what might be inside the package; then open the gift to reveal the book. After reading the book aloud, encourage each student to share a favorite book from your classroom library with a friend.

22—Be An Angel Day

This day is set aside to "do one small act of service for someone." Invite each student to think of something nice she could do at home— such as cleaning her room or setting the table for dinner. Write each child's act of service on a slip of paper. Then have each child make an angel by accordion-folding a round doily. Secure the folds by wrapping a pipe cleaner around the middle. Instruct each child to draw an angel's face on a construction-paper circle. Glue the circle to the center of the folded doily. Attach the child-dictated slip of paper to the back of the angel. Encourage each child to take her angel home to share with her family, as a promise to do the described service.

26—First Baseball Games Televised: Anniversary

On this date in 1939, the first major-league baseball games were televised from Ebbets Field in New York City. Celebrate this occasion by dividing your students into two teams and playing a simplified game of baseball. If possible, videotape the game. Then serve peanuts and cold drinks as you play the tape for your youngsters. Your little rookies will feel like big-league players when they see their game on TV!

August

CLASSROOM NEWS

Teacher: _____ Date: _____

A Peek At The Week

Looking Ahead

Reminders

Special Thanks

Help Wanted

Sunny Sunflowers

Bring the golden glow of summer into your classroom with this bouquet of sunflower ideas. Your students will be blossoming with science, math, and language skills when you pick this summertime unit.

ideas contributed by Barbara Backer and Lori Kent

Budding Knowledge

Dig right into your sunflower study by reading aloud the book *Sunflower* by Miela Ford (Greenwillow Books). This book's simple text and bold illustrations will help your little ones understand the life cycle of a sunflower from seed to flower, then back to seed. After reading the story, share a real or an artifical sunflower with students. (Sunflower plants may be available at your local garden shop or home improvement store.) Encourage youngsters to notice the tiny florets in the flower head, and the many sunflower seeds hidden beneath them.

Total Recall

After completing the activity above, ask students to recall the various stages of sunflower growth. Then use the sequencing cards on page 12 to illustrate the following poem. Enlarge the cards if desired; then duplicate them onto tagboard. Color and cut out the cards; then back each card with felt. Teach students the following poem, using the appropriate cards to illustrate each stage. Then place the cards and a flannelboard in a learning center for students to use during free-choice time.

See my pretty sunflower
Standing oh, so tall.
It started from a seed—oh, so small.
(Use card 5.)

I planted it in soil,
In the bright sunshine.
I sprinkled it with water
And it grew just fine.
(Use card 1.)

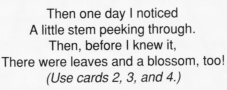

Then one day I noticed
A little stem peeking through.
Then, before I knew it,
There were leaves and a blossom, too!
(Use cards 2, 3, and 4.)

Now my flower's big and tall.
It looks up at the sun.
And tucked within its sunny face
Are seeds to eat—yum yum!
(Use card 5.)

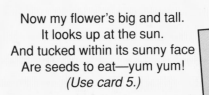

Bloomin' Blossom Booklet

This bloomin' blossom booklet is sure to help youngsters' sequencing skills grow and grow! For each child, duplicate the sequencing cards on page 12. Next duplicate the sunflower pattern on page 13 onto yellow construction paper. Then duplicate the stem pattern on page 14 onto green construction paper. Cut out the sunflower and stem pieces; then glue the pieces together as indicated.

To make a booklet, have a child glue sunflower seeds to the center of his sunflower cutout. While the glue is drying, have him cut out his sequencing cards. Direct him to sequence his cards, then glue each card in the designated space on the sunflower stem as shown. When the glue is dry, accordion-fold the stem; then attach a packet of seeds to the back of the sunflower cutout. Encourage each child to take his booklet home to share with his family.

Plant A Little Flower

Students' faces will bloom with delight when they see their tiny seeds sprout from these sunny containers. Duplicate a class supply of the sunflower and leaf patterns (page 13) onto yellow and green construction paper respectively. To make a sunflower, have each child paint a Styrofoam® cup with black tempera paint to which a drop of liquid detergent has been added. Have her cut out a sunflower and leaf pattern, then glue the leaf cutout to the underside of the sunflower cutout as shown. Invite the child to fill her cup with soil, then to plant a sunflower seed in the soil. Then help her to glue the bottom of the cup to the center of the flower. Place the containers near a sunny window, and mist them daily with a spritz of water. When the seeds begin to sprout, urge each child to take her sunny sprout home to plant in her yard!

Kathy Folz—Gr. K
South Elementary, Franklin Park, IL

From Seed To Flower

Now that youngsters know about the life cycle of a sunflower, introduce some sunflower-seed savvy with this activity. Explain to youngsters that some sunflower seeds are harvested for planting, and some are harvested for eating. Show students a package of sunflower seeds for planting. Have them observe the picture on the front of the package; then read aloud the planting instructions. Invite each youngster to take a seed and crack open the shell, noting the small kernel inside. Explain to students that the kernel is the part of the seed that will become the sunflower. (Warn students NOT to eat the seeds packaged for planting as they may have been treated with chemicals.)

Next show your youngsters seeds that are packaged for eating. Invite each child to take several seeds, then crack one open. Encourage students to notice that the planting seeds and the edible seeds look identical. After children have observed both types of seeds, invite them to crack open their remaining edible seeds and nibble away!

Bird "Tweets"

People aren't the only ones who love sunflower seeds—birds do, too! Youngsters will delight in making these whimsical bird feeders to give their feathered friends a yummy treat! Save milk cartons from school lunches until you have one clean, dry carton for each child. Cut off the top of each carton as shown. Cover the outside of each carton with a sunny sunflower or bright checked pattern of Con-Tact® covering. Punch four holes, one on each side of the carton. Thread a length of yarn through two opposite holes and tie it to create a loop. Then create a perch by inserting a pencil through the two remaining holes. Fill the cartons with sunflower birdseed; then hang them in a tree near your classroom windows. Tweet! Tweet!

Mask Appeal

Bright, shiny faces will bloom from the centers of these giant blossoms. To make one, cut out the center from a paper plate. Paint the plate brown. Sprinkle coffee grounds on the paint while it is wet to resemble the florets at a sunflower's center. Next cut or tear petals from bright yellow or gold tissue paper. When the paint is dry, glue the petals around the outer edge. Glue sunflower seeds around the opening and at the base of the petals. Staple or tape a wide craft stick to the bottom of the mask as shown. Use these sunny blossoms with the following activities.

As Big As A Sunflower

Your little sunflowers will grow tall when acting out this sunny poem. Use face paint to paint black, seed-shaped freckles on each child's' cheeks. Then have youngsters begin in a crouching position, holding their sunflower masks (see "Mask Appeal") in front of their faces. As you lead them in the following verse, encourage each child to slowly stand, then stretch up on tiptoes and reach for the sky.

Growing Tall
The yellow sunflower grows so high.
It almost seems to touch the sky.
Mother says I'm growing, too.
Sunflower, will I be as big as you?
—*Barbara Backer*

Fields Of Flowers

You'll see a field of sunny faces when youngsters use their sunflower masks to imitate the movements of a sunflower. Before beginning cut out a sun shape from a sheet of construction paper. Explain to students that sunflowers slowly move throughout the day so that their heads always face the sun.

Then invite little ones to hold their masks in front of their faces. While holding the sun cutout in front of you, move to various parts of the room. Encourage students to keep their feet planted in one place as they move their heads and bodies to face the sun cutout. Afterward lead your little blossoms in the following song:

(sung to the tune of "Clementine")
I'm a sunflower. I'm a sunflower.
I stand in the sun all day.
I sway in the gentle breezes,
And I face the sun always.

When the sun comes up each morning,
My head lifts to face the light.
I keep looking at the sunshine,
'Till I go to sleep at night.

9

A Bouquet Of Sunflower Centers

Sunflowers will be popping up all over when you enhance some of your learning centers with these ideas.

Tactile Center

Youngsters will love the feel of these black beauties! Visit a gardening center to purchase black sunflower-seed bird food. Then fill your tactile tub with the seeds and a collection of variously sized scoops. Little ones will enjoy exploring the silky texture of the seeds. Afterward, toss the seeds outside. The birds will thank you for such a nutty surprise!

Cooking Center

This edible sunflower looks almost too cute to eat. To make one, spread cream cheese that has been tinted yellow onto a round cracker. Sprinkle shelled sunflower seeds atop the cream cheese. Place triangular cheese crackers around the edge of the cracker to resemble petals. What a sunny delight!

Block Center

Add toy tractors, miniature gardening tools, a variety of small, silk or plastic sunflowers, and a few green Styrofoam® squares (available at craft stores) to your block area. Then invite students to create sunflower farms with the provided materials and their imaginations.

Math Center

Stock this center with edible sunflower seeds and a few colored copies of the counting mat on page 15. Encourage a child visiting this center to place seeds atop the seed shapes on each sunflower. When all the shapes are covered, direct him to count the number of seeds on each flower. When he finishes counting, he may crack open and eat his sunflower-seed counters. Yummy!

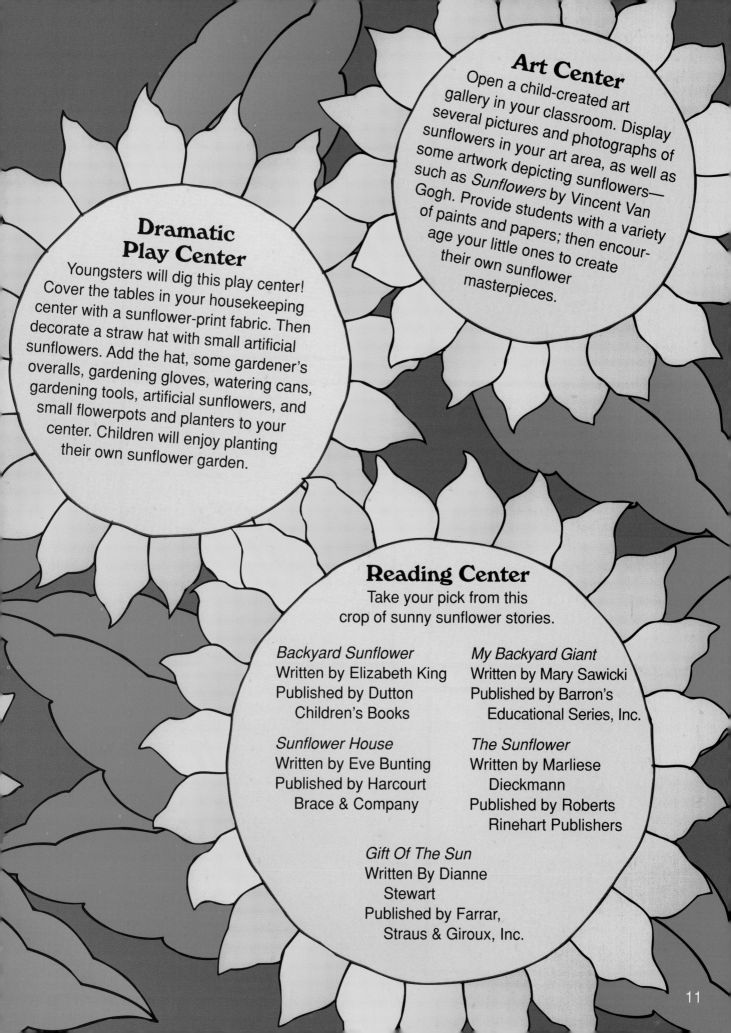

Art Center

Open a child-created art gallery in your classroom. Display several pictures and photographs of sunflowers in your art area, as well as some artwork depicting sunflowers—such as *Sunflowers* by Vincent Van Gogh. Provide students with a variety of paints and papers; then encourage your little ones to create their own sunflower masterpieces.

Dramatic Play Center

Youngsters will dig this play center! Cover the tables in your housekeeping center with a sunflower-print fabric. Then decorate a straw hat with small artificial sunflowers. Add the hat, some gardener's overalls, gardening gloves, watering cans, gardening tools, artificial sunflowers, and small flowerpots and planters to your center. Children will enjoy planting their own sunflower garden.

Reading Center

Take your pick from this crop of sunny sunflower stories.

Backyard Sunflower
Written by Elizabeth King
Published by Dutton
Children's Books

My Backyard Giant
Written by Mary Sawicki
Published by Barron's
Educational Series, Inc.

Sunflower House
Written by Eve Bunting
Published by Harcourt
Brace & Company

The Sunflower
Written by Marliese
Dieckmann
Published by Roberts
Rinehart Publishers

Gift Of The Sun
Written By Dianne
Stewart
Published by Farrar,
Straus & Giroux, Inc.

Sequencing Cards

Use with "Total Recall" on page 6 and "Bloomin' Blossom Booklet" on page 7.

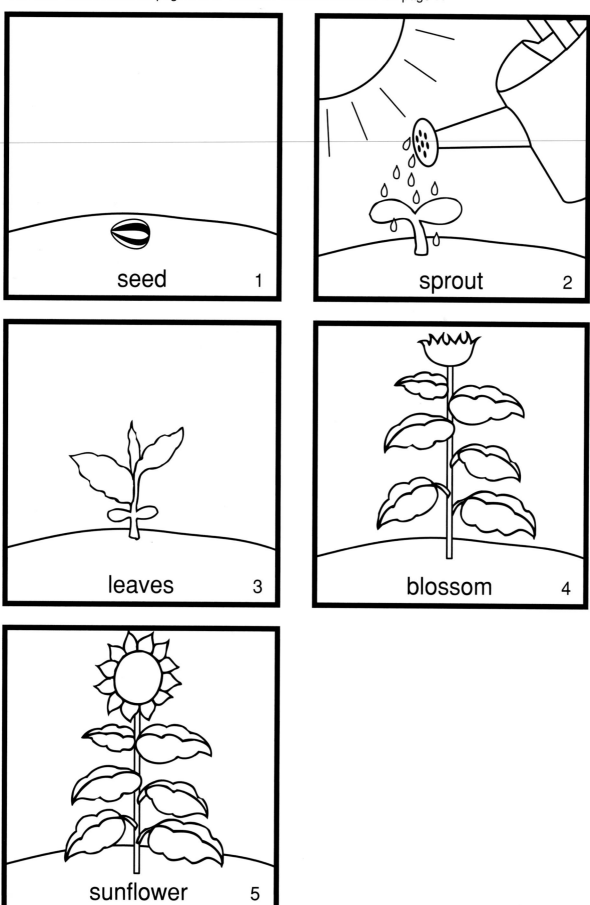

seed   1

sprout   2

leaves   3

blossom   4

sunflower   5

Sunflower And Leaf Patterns
Use with "Bloomin' Blossom Booklet" and
"Plant A Little Flower" on page 7.

13

Stem Pattern

Use with "Bloomin' Blossom Booklet" on page 7.

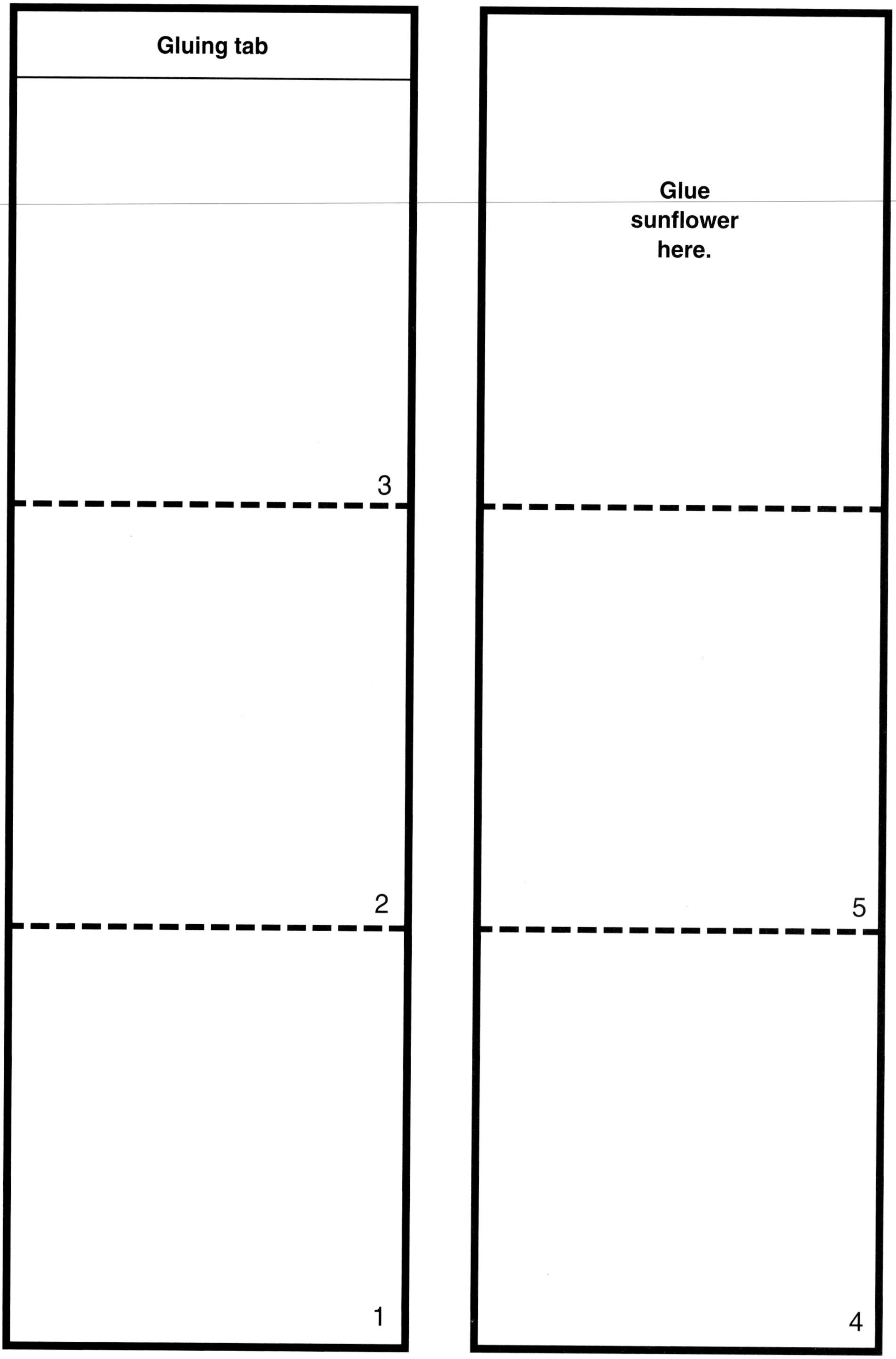

Gluing tab

**Glue
sunflower
here.**

3

2

1

5

4

In Praise Of Pets

A pet and a child make a perfect pair! Teach your little ones about kindness and responsibility with this unit in praise of pets.

ideas by Linda Blassingame, Jayne Gammons, and Lori Kent

What Is A Pet?

Begin your pet ponderings by providing youngsters with a collection of magazines containing pictures of both wild and domestic animals. Ask the children to find and cut out animal pictures. When each child has cut out several pictures, gather the children together for a group time. Ask students to answer the question, "What is a pet?" Record their answers on a bulletin-board-paper house shape. Then explain that a pet is an animal kept for pleasure, usually in a home or in a yard. Further explain that pets must be fed, groomed, regularly taken to a veterinarian, and loved. Then, as a group, look at the pictures and decide which animals would make the best pets. Glue the pictures that the group selects around the comments on the house shape. Keep the remaining pictures for use in "Our Class Pet."

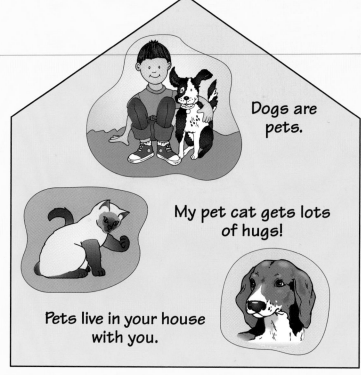

Dogs are pets.

My pet cat gets lots of hugs!

Pets live in your house with you.

Did we get a lion?

No! A lion has big teeth.

Did we get a guinea pig?

Yes! We can keep him in a cage. We can hold him.

Our Class Pet

If you don't already have one, now's the perfect time to purchase a classroom critter! Make a list of the types of pets your children own, adding any other animals that are common pets. As a group discuss the care and type of surroundings that each animal requires. Then decide which animal would make the best pet for your class. When the group has reached a consensus, ask for parents' support in buying the animal and setting up its new home. Take a picture of the pet; then use the picture and the wild-animal pictures collected in "What Is A Pet?" to create a class book.

Title a large construction-paper cover "Our Class Pet." Program the first page to read "Our class wanted a pet." Glue each of the wild-animal pictures onto a separate sheet of paper. Program each page as shown, substituting youngsters' thoughts as to why each different animal would be an unacceptable pet. Glue the picture of your class pet to the final page, programming the page with reasons why the pet was chosen for adoption. Bind the pages together to complete a class book that's sure to be "pet-ticularly" popular!

Pet Preferences

There's a perfect pet for every personality. Find out your students' pet preferences; then use the results for some math fun. Informally poll individual children to find out which pet from the selections on pages 22 and 23 they would choose to own. Based on students' choices, duplicate onto construction paper the appropriate number of each pattern. Direct each child to color and cut out his pattern; then staple it onto a personalized sentence-strip headband. During one or more group times, ask each child to wear his headband. Then choose from the following activities:

Sights And Sounds

Ask the group to sort themselves by the pet preferences displayed on their headbands. For added fun have each child move and make the sounds associated with his animal to help in finding the members of his group.

"Purr-fect" Patterning

Line up a number of students so that the pets displayed on their headbands create a pattern. Once the pattern has been identified by the remainder of the class, have each child from left to right in the line make her animal's sound or movement.

"Grrr-eat" Graphing

On a length of bulletin-board paper, create a floor graph with two columns. Assign a pet label to each column. To graph students' pet choices, direct students wearing the corresponding headbands to stand on the graph. Record the results of each graph you create.

meow meow

ruff ruff

squeak squeak

susan hodnett

My Pet And Me

Owning a pet is a lot of fun, but it's also a lot of responsibility! Use this booklet idea to teach your little ones about a pet's basic needs. For each child duplicate pages 24 and 25; then cut the pages apart on the dotted lines. Glue the last page to the center of a red tagboard heart. Stack the pet pages in order; then staple them to the tagboard along the left side of the last page. Stack the child pages in order; then staple them to the tagboard along the right side of the last page. Have a child write (or dictate) his completion to the sentence on each page. (If the child does not have a pet, encourage him to write about a pet he would like to have.) If desired glue a photo of the child with his pet to the last page of the booklet. Then direct the child to illustrate the pages. My pet and I need the same thing—each other!

Woof, Meow, Squeak

In case your little ones haven't noticed yet, pets have feelings too! Animals use sounds and body movements to communicate their needs and moods. Use the following song and actions to get youngsters moving and "talking" like the animals.

Pet Talk

(sung to the tune of "Itsy-Bitsy Spider")

A very happy puppy wags its tail like this.	*Pause to "wag tail."*
Then, with its tongue, it gives your hand a kiss!	*Pretend to lick.*
If it is scared, it barks or starts to growl.	*Bark and growl.*
But to tell you that it loves you, a puppy says, "Bow wow!"	*Say, "Bow wow!"*
A very happy kitten rubs and starts to purr.	*Pause to rub ear with "paw."*
If it is scared, it raises up its fur.	*Raise shoulders.*
Then it will hiss and crinkle up its brow.	*Hiss and crinkle brow.*
But to tell you that it loves you, a kitten says, "Meow!"	*Say, "Meow!"*
A very happy hamster likes to run and hide.	*Pause to run in place.*
If it is scared, it leans over to one side.	*Lean to one side.*
It pulls in its paws and only looks to peek.	*Hide face under "paws."*
But to tell you that it loves you, a hamster says, "Squeak, squeak!"	*Say, "Squeak, squeak."*

Puppy Love

Buried Treasure

Burying and digging up treats is a favorite pastime of man's best friend. Prepare this center so your little ones can bone up on counting and number sets. Duplicate ten dog patterns (page 22) onto construction paper. Label each dog with a different numeral from one to ten. Cut out each dog pattern; then tape it to a resealable plastic bag. Hide 55 Milkbone® dog bones in your sensory table's sand. To use the center, a child digs in the sand to retrieve the bones. He then fills each bag with the corresponding number of bones. Now that's doggone fun!

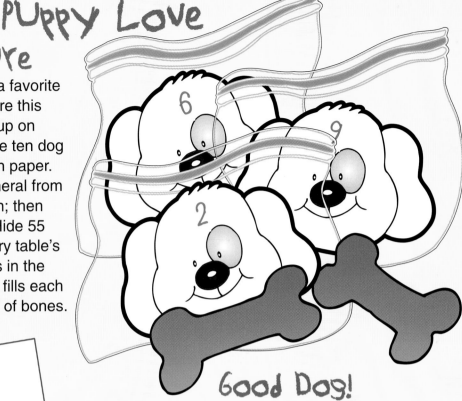

Good Dog!

Teach youngsters some new tricks with this canine role-playing activity. Program individual index cards with dog commands—such as *fetch, sit, lie down, roll over, bark, beg,* and *come*—and corresponding picture cues. Give one child in a pair the set of cards. Encourage him to show his partner a card and read the command. His partner pretends to be the dog and performs the trick. When all of the commands have been read and performed, the partners switch roles. Ready for a treat?

fetch

roll over

sit

"Paws" For Reading

I Really Want A Dog
Written by Susan Breslow and Sally Blakemore
Published by Puffin Books

Any Kind Of Dog
Written by Lynn Reiser
Published by Greenwillow Books

I'll Always Love You
Written by Hans Wilhelm
Published by Crown Books For Young Readers

The Cat's Meow

Cool Collars

Youngsters will feel like fancy felines when wearing these captivating cat collars. To make a collar, direct a child to cut through a paper plate's rim to its center, then cut out the center of the plate. Next have him paint the resulting collar. When the paint is dry, personalize the collar with the cat name the child would like to be called. Then invite him to decorate his collar with a variety of craft materials such as sequins, fake jewels, beads, pom-poms, and jingle bells. Here, kitty, kitty!

Kitty-Cat "Crunchies"

Entice your litter with this cat snack. For each child personalize a paper bowl with her chosen cat name (see "Cool Collars"). Have each student decorate her bowl with a variety of cat-related stickers; then invite her to prepare a snack of Kitty-Cat "Crunchies" by combining equal portions of fish crackers, triangular crackers, and pretzel sticks in her bowl. Serve the snacks with cups of milk. These treats are sure to leave your little kittens meowing for more!

Catnap

Prepare your students for catnaps and a cat tale with some of these soothing cat movements. Have students stretch like cats by arching their backs and dropping their hands down to their feet. Next have students lie on the floor and roll their bodies into balls, then stretch their bodies out long and lean. Finally have students curl up in a group area while you read a book aloud. "Purr-fect!"

Cat Tales

Have You Seen My Cat?
Written by Eric Carle
Published by Scholastic Inc.

My New Kitten
Written by Joanna Cole
Published by Morrow Junior Books

The Tenth Good Thing About Barney
Written by Judith Viorst
Published by Atheneum Books For Young Readers

The Age Of Aquariums

Your little ones are just the right age to enjoy this fishy water-center idea. Gather the listed items and place them near your filled water table. Encourage youngsters who visit the center to arrange the gravel and aquatic items in the water to "set up" the aquarium. Invite youngsters to use the net to catch fish put in the water. If desired explain that when a pet fish is brought to a new aquarium, it needs time to adjust to the temperature of that aquarium's water. To demonstrate how to care for a new fish, put a plastic fish in a clear bag filled with water. Tie the top of the bag; then let the bag float in the water table until the pet fish "adjusts" to its new home. Also demonstrate how to use the thermometer to check the water temperature. During cleanup time, have a child fill the sieve with the gravel and replace the gravel in the bucket. Provide towels for drying the remaining aquatic items.

aquarium gravel in a bucket
sieve
shells
plastic plants
landscaping pieces
plastic fish
small net
water thermometer
towels

Pennies For Pets

Conclude your unit with a project that you can count on to foster kindness for our animal friends. Explain that many animals that do not have homes live in animal shelters. Further explain that workers at shelters care for homeless pets while seeking good homes for the animals. Suggest that the class donate pennies to help a local organization care for animals until they are adopted as pets. Send home duplicated copies of the parent note (page 23) explaining the project. Use construction paper to decorate an empty facial-tissue box to resemble a dog or cat. As students bring in donations, have them drop the pennies into the decorated box. After a desired amount of time, have children help to roll the pennies. Then plan a class trip to the chosen organization to deliver the donation. If a trip is not possible, deliver the donation to the shelter and take several pictures of the site to help the children understand how their pennies will help pets.

Pet Patterns

Use with "Pet Preferences" on page 17. Use the dog pattern also with "Buried Treasure" on page 19.

Pet Patterns
Use with "Pet Preferences" on page 17.

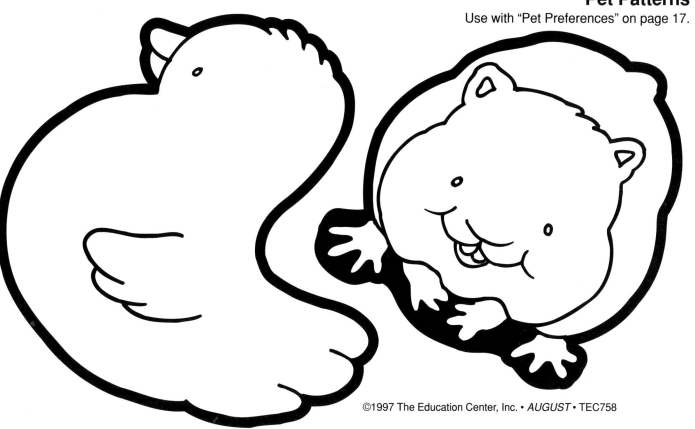

Parent Note
Use with "Pennies For Pets" on page 21.

Dear Families,

Please help us with a new project—Pennies For Pets. During our pet unit, we have learned that animals need food, shelter, and love. We will collect pennies until _____ to
(date)
help _____ care for and
(organization)
find homes for pets.

Woof, woof! Meow!
(Thank you!)

_____'s class
(teacher)

My Pet

And Me

My pet's name is

_____.

My name is

_____.

My pet needs food.

I need food.

It eats _____.

I eat _____.

1

1

My pet needs shelter.

I need shelter.

It lives in _____.

2

I live at _____.

2

My pet needs love.

I love my pet!

3

From Lemons To Lemonade

When life gives you lemons, make it a learning experience! Use this collection of cross-curricular ideas to bring the summertime fun of ice-cold lemonade into your classroom. *by Stacie Davis*

Citrus "Sense-ations"

Begin this unit by surveying students to determine how many of them have ever tasted lemonade. Afterward show your little ones some real lemons and explain that this fruit is an important ingredient in good old-fashioned lemonade. Then encourage youngsters to explore this citrus fruit with all five senses. Begin by posting a bulletin-board-paper chart similar to the one shown. Then ask questions such as, "What does a lemon look like?" and "How does a lemon feel?" Cut the lemons into bite-size wedges and ask children to tell you how the lemon smells. Invite interested students to taste their lemon wedges. As children explore the lemons, record their responses on the chart. Conclude the lesson by asking students to reflect on the similarities and differences between lemons and lemonade.

A lemon looks ...
yellow   like a lime

A lemon feels...
smooth   squishy
             inside

A lemon smells...
strong   like an
              orange

A lemon tastes...
SOUR!   good

A lemon sounds...
It doesn't make
any noise.

Making Lemonade

Teach your students this action song to help them understand how lemonade is made.

This Is The Way We Make Lemonade
(sung to the tune of "Here We Go 'Round The Mulberry Bush")

This is the way we make lemonade,
Make lemonade, make lemonade.
This is the way we make lemonade,
On a summer morning.

This is the way we cut the lemons,
Cut the lemons, cut the lemons.
This is the way we cut the lemons,
On a summer morning.

Hold one palm flat; use other hand to show cutting motion.

This is the way we squeeze the juice,
Squeeze the juice, squeeze the juice.
This is the way we squeeze the juice,
On a summer morning.

Clench fingers as if squeezing; then twist wrist repeatedly.

Next we add the sugar and water,
Sugar and water, sugar and water.
Next we add the sugar and water,
On a summer morning.

Pretend to pour in sugar and water; then stir.

This is the way we drink lemonade,
Drink lemonade, drink lemonade.
This is the way we drink lemonade,

Pretend to drink from a glass.

Kimberly Richard

26 On a summer morning.

Give It A Squeeze, Please

Are your little ones ready for a drink of lemonade? If so enlist their help in juicing lemons to be used in making lemonade. Begin by cutting each of five lemons in half or in quarters so that each child has a section of lemon to squeeze. Explain to students that to make two quarts of lemonade, they'll need one cup of lemon juice. Show students a one-cup measuring cup and ask them if they think that the juice squeezed from all their lemon sections combined will be less than, more than, or equal to one cup. Then let the squeezing begin! Encourage each student in turn to squeeze her lemon's juice into a widemouthed glass container. After each child has had a turn, carefully remove any seeds using a slotted spoon. (If desired, save the seeds for use with "A Slice Of Summer" on page 29.) Pour the accumulated lemon juice into the cup to measure the results. Reserve the juice for the next activity.
(Note: Five lemons should yield approximately one cup of juice. For better results, leave the fruit at room temperature for 30 minutes prior to juicing; then roll each lemon on a counter or tabletop under the palm of your hand.)

Luscious Lemonade

Now that the juice has been squeezed, you're ready to make lemonade! In a two-quart pitcher, mix one cup of lemon juice and one cup of sugar with six and one-half cups of ice-cold water. If desired put some lemon slices in the pitcher as well. Give each child a serving of lemonade in a disposable cup. After your students have enjoyed their lemonade, teach them the chant below. Encourage students to replace the boldfaced word with another adjective—such as *cool, delicious,* or *refreshing*—each time the chant is repeated.

Lemonade, lemonade,
In my cup.
It tasted so **good**,
I drank it all up!

Lemonade Sequencing

Use this nifty necklace project to sequence the steps followed to make lemonade. To make a necklace, each student will need a yellow construction-paper copy of the patterns on page 30, scissors, access to a hole puncher, and a 30-inch length of yellow yarn. (Tape one end of each yarn length for easier lacing). Have each student cut out his construction-paper lemon slices; then assist him in punching two holes in each cutout as indicated. Next instruct each student to place his yarn flat on his desk. Invite children to look at the text and drawing on each of the lemon slices and determine which lemon slice should be first. To make sure the lemon slices are sequenced correctly, have each student thread the slices from right to left. Finish the necklace by tying a knot in the yarn. Encourage students to wear their necklaces home and "read" them to family members.

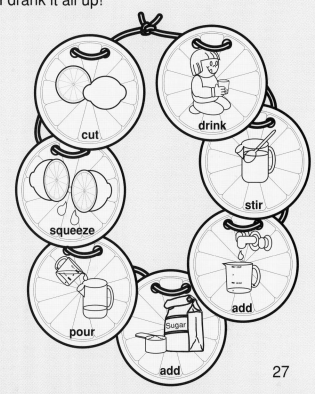

27

Which Flavor Do You Favor?

Which type of lemonade do your students like best? Find out when you put your little consumers' taste buds to work with this lemonade-tasting activity. In advance prepare a variety of lemonade flavors, such as yellow lemonade, pink lemonade, and raspberry or strawberry lemonade. Or prepare several different *kinds* of lemonade, such as lemonade made from a powdered mix, lemonade made from frozen concentrate, and fresh-squeezed lemonade. Also prepare a graph similar to the one shown. Then have your students sample each of the different kinds of lemonade. Afterward give each student a lemon-shaped cutout on which his name has been printed. Invite each student to place his lemon cutout on the graph to indicate which type of lemonade he prefers. Be sure to discuss the concepts of *more, fewer,* and *equal* as you count the votes.

Pinky Pink Lemonade	Sue	David	Tia			
Country Acres Lemonade	Kevin	Lu				
Fresh and Frosty Lemonade	Polly	Jen	Chan	John		
Mrs. Davis's Fresh-Squeezed Lemonade	Tim	Mia	Juan	Ada	Franz	Kelly

A Sidewalk Café

Transform your dramatic-play area into a sidewalk café where all types of lemonade are served. Begin by covering a table with a red checkered tablecloth. Set a few chairs around the table so that patrons have a place to sit. Provide aprons for the waiters and waitresses to wear, and be sure to have several (empty) plastic pitchers of "lemonade" on hand. Provide the waiters and waitresses with trays, plastic glasses, a toy cash register, and notepads so that they can write down orders. Engage youngsters in creating signs and price lists for the cafe. Each day invite a different group of students to visit the center. May I refill your glass for you, sir?

Lemonade Cafe

Paint "Scent-sations"

Mix up a batch of this "scent-sational" paint for some projects that smell as good as they look! To make the paint, mix one-half cup of cold water with a three-ounce package of lemon-flavored gelatin. Use this paint for the activities described below.

We Love Lemonade!

Add a touch of summertime fun to your class-room with this creative bulletin-board idea. Begin by giving each child a yellow cutout in the shape of a drinking glass. Have each student paint her glass cutout with the "scent-sational" paint. While the paint is drying, provide each student with a sheet of flesh-colored construction paper. Help each student trace her hands on the paper; then have her cut out the hands. Next invite each child to use fabric scraps, construction paper, yarn, markers, and glue to create a self-likeness on a nine-inch paper plate. When the paint on the glass cutout has dried, tape a plastic straw to the back of the cutout. Finally, have each student assemble her project on a sheet of 12" x 18" construction paper as shown. Staple the completed projects to a bulletin board titled "We Love Lemonade!"

A Slice Of Summer

Any way you slice this activity, the results are fun! For each child trace and cut around a six-inch paper plate to create a yellow, construction-paper circle; then use a perma-nent marker to make the circle resemble a lemon slice. Invite each student to use a cotton swab to paint the inside of each section on his lemon-slice cutout with the "scent-sational" paint. After the cutout has dried, give each student a few clean lemon seeds that he can glue to his lemon-slice cutout. Then invite each student to dictate a sentence about why he likes summer. Use a marker to write the student's dictation around the edge of his lemon slice. Mount the completed projects on a bulletin board titled "A Slice Of Summer."

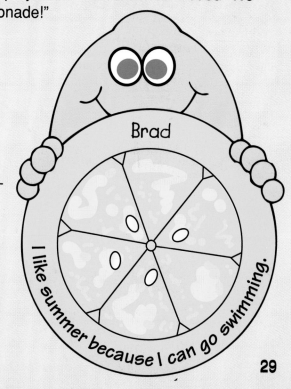

Brad

I like summer because I can go swimming.

29

Necklace Patterns

Use with "Lemonade Sequencing" on page 27.

cut

squeeze

add

pour

add

drink

stir

Up, Up, And Away With Balloons

This collection of balloon ideas is sure to be "pop-ular" with your students.

ideas contributed by Mackie Rhodes and dayle timmons

Let's Go Fly A...Balloon!

Use this high-flying experiment to introduce youngsters to two types of balloons—air-filled and helium-filled. In advance obtain a helium-filled rubber balloon; then inflate another rubber balloon by mouth or with a balloon pump. Tie the loose end of a separate roll of kite string to each balloon; then reel the string tightly around the roll. While outdoors show the balloons to your class. Ask students to predict whether or not each balloon will float when its string is unwrapped. Then have volunteers slowly unwrap the strings attached to the balloons. What happens? Explain to students that the balloon that drops to the ground is filled with regular air, but the floating balloon is filled with a gas called *helium.* Since helium is lighter than air, it causes the balloon to float.

Afterward invite students to take turns flying each of the balloons as if flying a kite. Encourage them to experiment with the flight patterns of each balloon by running in different directions and releasing, then reeling in, the string to different lengths.

Staying Afloat

Youngsters will discover the buoyancy of air-filled and helium-filled balloons when they try this activity. Put some small, inflated balloons in a filled water table or wading pool. Invite youngsters to attempt to submerge the balloons. What happens? Lead students to discover that the air inside the balloons enables them to stay afloat.

After youngsters discuss their discoveries, equate the air-filled balloons with swimming floats and rafts. Explain that the air inside the inflatables enables them to stay afloat and support the weight of the users. Encourage each youngster to share this information with a pool buddy during his next swimming excursion.

Note: Balloons can be a choking hazard for small children. In addition the sound of a popping balloon may frighten some children. Please supervise students closely during all balloon activities.

Gotta Dance!

These dancing partners will bring out the rhythm in even your most reserved youngsters. If possible obtain a helium-filled balloon on a string for each child. Or give each child an air-filled balloon. Tie a loop in the end of each string to create a handle for the balloon. Then instruct each child to carefully draw a face on her balloon using a permanent marker. If desired have her glue or tape accordion-folded construction-paper strips to the balloon head to represent arms and legs. After youngsters complete their balloon people, play some lively dancing music; then invite each child to dance with her balloon creature. Just a-movin' and a-groovin' to the beat!

Shoot Two

Youngsters will get plenty of practice in eye-hand coordination when they play this balloon-style game of shooting hoops. Create a modified basketball goal by positioning a large plastic hoop over the backs of two chairs. If necessary secure the hoop to each chair with a length of rope. Then attach a beanbag to a short length of a string tied to a helium-filled balloon. Inflate another balloon by mouth or with a balloon pump; then knot the balloon. Explain to students that the air-filled balloon can be tossed into the hoop like a basketball, but the helium-filled balloon—because of its lighter-than-air property—must be thrown by an attached weight: the beanbag.

To play have each child, in turn, attempt to throw each balloon through the hoop from a designated distance. Then encourage him to share his observations about throwing each balloon. Two points!

The Thrill Of Suspense

Here's another fun challenge to hone youngsters' eye-hand skills. Tie a separate helium-filled balloon to each of three chairs so that the balloons are freely suspended in the air. Then create a clothesline at or above a child's height. Use spring-type clothespins to attach the strings of several air-filled balloons so that they are suspended from the line. To play give a child a supply of beanbags; then encourage her to try to hit each of the balloons with a beanbag. At the end of her turn, ask her which type of balloon was easiest to hit. To extend this activity, challenge the student to identify the targeted balloon before she throws the beanbag. Ooooh, the thrill of suspense!

Funny-Bones Freeze

This game of giggles and guffaws will have you wondering if youngsters' funny bones are really attached to a balloon. Gather youngsters into a spacious area. Show them an air-filled balloon, explaining that it is filled with an imaginary laughing gas. When you give the balloon a boost of gas—or a toss high into the air—students will engage in loud laughter and general silliness. As the balloon descends, give it additional boosts while encouraging youngsters to adjust their activity to match the height of the balloon in the air. Then allow the balloon to finally land on the ground. At this time each youngster will freeze into a silent, still position until you boost the balloon with another shot of imaginary laughing gas. It's the funny-bones freeze!

Bursting With Pride

Students will feel a great sense of pride when they complete this balloon obstacle course. To prepare collect a class supply of various small toy prizes or individually wrapped snacks. Then insert a rolled slip of paper labeled with one of the prizes or snacks into a balloon for each child. Blow up and knot each balloon. Arrange a simple obstacle course in your school's gym or an outdoor play area. Then give each child a balloon. Encourage each child in turn to gently kick her balloon through the course, being careful not to pop it. Then, at the end of the course, ask the child to celebrate her accomplishment by popping her balloon by any means she chooses—stomping on it, sitting on it, or poking it with a pointed object. Invite her to collect the prize printed on the paper slip inside her balloon. She'll be bursting with pride!

Balloons À La Cream

Here's a "sense-ational" activity designed to promote youngsters' fine-motor skills. Give each child an inflated balloon with an attached spring-type clothespin to serve as a handle. Spray a small amount of shaving cream on the child's balloon; then have him spread the cream over the surface of his balloon. Encourage him to use his finger or a craft stick to draw designs in the cream. To erase, have him smooth the cream with his flattened hand; then invite him to create another creamy design.

Everybody Loves A Clown

…and balloons! That's why balloons and clowns are naturals together. Invite youngsters to create one of these balloon-clown crafts; then invite them to clown around with their creations for some dramatic-play fun.

- To make a clown mask, help each child cut eye holes in a paper plate. Then invite him to use crayons and craft materials to decorate the plate to resemble a clown's face. Blow up and knot a small balloon. Poke a hole in the mask nose; then push the knotted end of the balloon through the hole. Tape the knot to the back of the mask. Attach the mask to a wide craft stick. Invite small groups of students to create clown skits to perform for the class.

- To make a balloon clown, inflate and knot a large balloon. Have each youngster dot an inverted paper plate with sticker dots, bingo daubers, circle stamps, or any other round print. Cut around the edges of the dotted plate to create a decorative clown collar. Poke a small hole in the middle of the collar; then insert the knotted end of the balloon through the hole. Secure the knot to the back of the collar with tape. Invite each child to design a clown face on the balloon using permanent markers, sticker dots, and construction-paper scraps and tape. If desired she may attach a decorated construction-paper hat to the top of her clown's head. Encourage youngsters to use their balloon clowns in dramatic-play activities—such as holding an imaginary circus, setting up housekeeping with a clown family, or having silly clowns visit a sick child. While not in use, the balloon clowns may be displayed around the room on shelves, window ledges, and tabletops.

This balloon made a dog.
Bobby

Clowning Around With Balloons

Fascinate youngsters with the exciting creations that can be made from balloons. If possible invite a balloon sculptor—one who twists and converts balloons into amazing creations—to visit your class. Or obtain a balloon pump and a bag of sculpting balloons; then teach yourself how to create balloon sculptures. If desired ask your visitor to arrive dressed as a clown. (If you are the sculptor, come to class dressed for the part.)

Then gather your students to witness the transformation of simple balloons into fun, functional, and decorative creations. Invite youngsters' comments on their observations. Afterward encourage each student to illustrate the first and the final stages of a balloon sculpture. Write his dictation about the sculpture on his paper; then bind all the pages into a class book titled "Our Balloon Creations." Share the book with the class, inviting each child to tell the class about his page. Then place the book in the reading center for individual students to enjoy.

The Great Balloon Challenge

Challenge youngsters to try some of these fun balloon activities.

- Set a timer for up to one minute. Encourage students to keep their balloons in the air until the timer bell rings—using only one body part, such as a hand, foot, or head.

- Ask youngsters to count the number of taps it takes to keep their balloons afloat during a timed period.

- Have students toss their balloons into the air, then clap their hands as many times as possible before catching their descending balloons.

- Challenge each child to spin around before catching a tossed balloon.

- Invite youngsters to count the number of stomps needed to burst their balloons.

Pam Crane

Stress Balloons

Just handling balloons has an amazing stress-reducing impact! Youngsters will be delighted to share some of this stress-relieving power with their families using these special balloons. To make a stress balloon, insert a plastic funnel into the mouth of a large, round party balloon. Fill the balloon with sand; then slip the balloon off the funnel and knot it. Use a length of curling ribbon to attach a copy of this rhyme to each stress balloon; then invite each child to take one home to her family.

When stress is filling up your world,
Give this balloon a squeeze.
And when your stress is all squeezed out,
Give me a hug-squeeze, please!

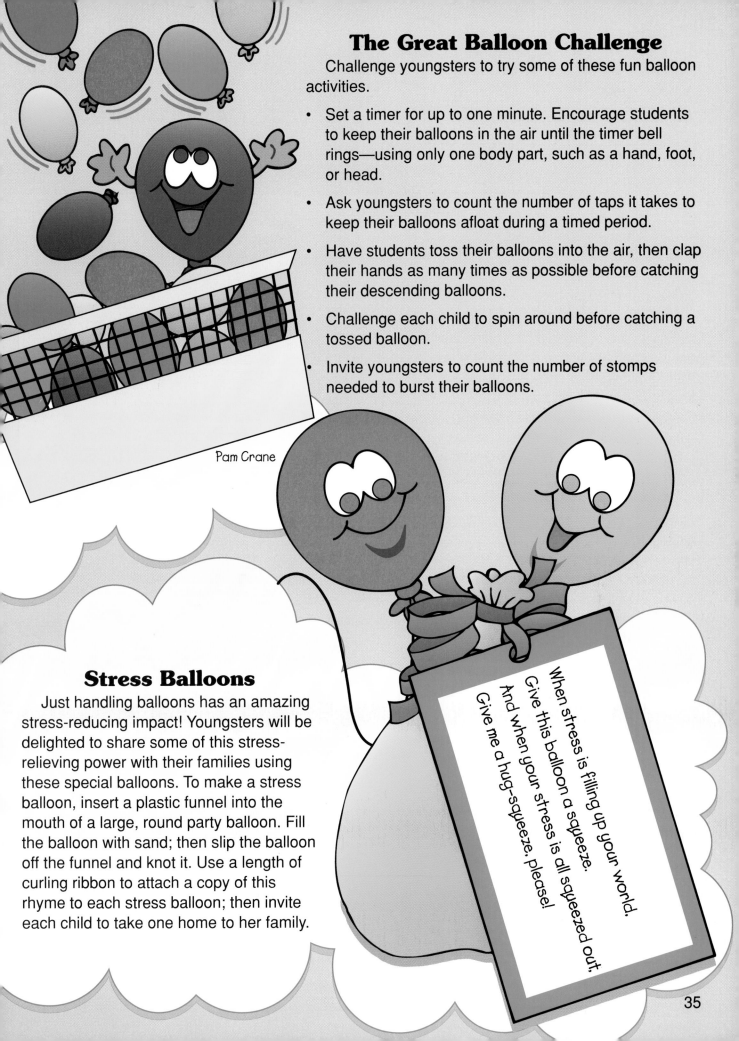

In The Green Grass

As the green grass grows, so will your little ones' learning with this patch of classy, grassy ideas!

ideas contributed by Christina McElhoes Yuhouse

Get Into It

Begin your unit by having youngsters get right into the grass! In advance locate a patch of grass near your classroom that is free from any dangers to bare feet, such as stinging ants or sharp twigs. Then take little ones outside to this location with snacks and books in hand. Seat them in a circle. Bring along a camera and enough film to photograph each child individually. Invite youngsters to remove their shoes and socks and let the grass tickle their toes while they enjoy their snacks, talk, or look at books.

Then inform your little ones that they're sitting right in the middle of your next unit of study—grass! Encourage them to use their senses and discuss the way the grass looks, feels, and smells. Before leaving your patch of green, invite each child to demonstrate a favorite grassy activity—such as lying back to observe the clouds, rolling through the soft grass, or just sitting quietly with a book—as you take her photograph. Once the photos are developed, glue each one to a separate sheet of construction paper and add a descriptive sentence as shown. Bind the completed pages together between construction-paper covers and add the title "In The Grass." Share the book with your class; then place it in your reading area for students to enjoy.

Mary Kay likes to dance in the grass.

A Gallery Of Grass Facts

- There are about 10,000 kinds of grass.
- Many kinds of plants belong to the grass family—including rice, wheat, corn, oats, barley, rye, bamboo, and sugarcane.
- Grass helps protect the soil. Its roots keep the soil particles together so they can't blow away on a windy day or wash away when it rains.
- Many animals—including cattle, goats, horses, and sheep—eat grasses as their main source of food.

Lawn Limerick

Help your students learn all about growing grass when you teach them this simple fingerplay.

If you want to grow grass on the ground,
Start by spreading some seeds all around.
Add a little light,

And water just right,
And before your eyes, grass will abound!

Point to the ground.
Pretend to sprinkle seeds.
Form sun with arms in circle
   overhead.
Wiggle fingers to show rain.
Point to eyes; then spread arms
   wide.

SEEDS

Grassy "Guess-timates"

After learning the "Lawn Limerick," your youngsters will be anxious to sprinkle a few *real* grass seeds and watch them grow. Purchase some quick-sprouting grass seed from your local garden shop or home-improvement store. Invite each child to fill a margarine tub with potting soil, sprinkle a small spoonful of grass seed on top, and water the seeds with a light misting from a spray bottle. Have students continue to water the seeds daily. (The seeds should sprout in about a week.)

Once the seeds have sprouted, ask little ones to estimate how high their grass will grow. Duplicate the measuring reproducible on page 42 for each child; then have each child cut along the bold lines and glue his reproducible to a craft stick. Ask him to mark a crayon line to show his estimate. Designate a day on which to check the grass height—such as after five or ten days. Have youngsters use their reproducible rulers to check and mark the actual height of their grass plants. Did anyone make an accurate guess? Did more children guess too high or too low?

Watch The

Green Grass Grow

5
4
3
2
1

The Parts Of The Plant

Pull up and bring in a clump of uncut grass from your yard, or ask your school or center director if you can mark off an area on your playground to remain uncut for several days. Have youngsters observe the parts of an uprooted grass plant, from the roots to the seed clusters that have formed. Then duplicate and prepare the patterns on pages 42 and 43 for flannelboard use. Teach youngsters this poem, displaying each flannelboard piece as indicated.

What is a grass plant? How will I know
All of the parts that help it to grow?

The roots are first; they grow in a bunch.   *Place root bunch on board.*
They drink up water and feed the plant lunch.

Next is the stem. It stands straight and tall.   *Fasten stem above root*
It's there so the rest of the plant does not fall.   *bunch.*

Then there are blades. They are thin and green—   *Attach four blades to*
The skinniest leaves you've ever seen!   *stem as shown.*

And last, but not least, there are spikelets on top.   *Add spikelets to top of stem.*
They hold the plant seeds 'til they're ready to drop.

Learning about grass can be easy and fun.
You now know its parts, so remember each one!   *Point to and review each part.*

Green Magic

Help youngsters discover the substance that makes grass green with this project. In advance cut a six-inch square of white fabric from an old cotton bedsheet for each child. You'll also need some flat pieces of wood and some smooth stones. When you're ready to begin, take little ones outside and ask them to collect some green plant samples, such as blades of grass, dandelion leaves, or clover. (Be sure to check your sample area ahead of time to be sure there aren't any poisonous plants around.) Have the children bring their samples back to your classroom. Ask a child to lay his samples on a piece of wood, cover them with his fabric square, and then tap the cloth firmly with a stone. Ta da! Magical green prints! If desired showcase the finished prints by mounting them on larger squares of green poster board for display.

After every child has had a turn to create an impressive impression, discuss what caused the green prints. Introduce the term *chlorophyll* and give a simple explanation of its purpose—to make food for the plant.

Who Goes There?

Lots of little critters make their homes in the grass. Explore the many inhabitants of a patch of grass by sharing *In The Tall, Tall Grass* by Denise Fleming (Henry Holt And Company, Inc.). Afterward provide your little ones with hand lenses and take them on a trip to a grassy play area to hunt for living creatures. Remind them to simply look at—but not disturb—any critters they find.

Then extend this lesson to the classroom by transforming your sensory table into a patch of grass. Fill your table with about two inches of potting soil. Top the soil with green Easter grass or green shredded paper to simulate grass. Toss in some plastic bugs, rubber fishing worms, or other grass-dwelling look-alikes you can find. Finally, add some sand-pail shovels and invite youngsters to explore. They'll dig this center!

Snakes In The Grass

Slither into fine-motor skills with this cutting and weaving activity. Have students recall some of the animals they've observed or discussed that live in the grass (see "Who Goes There?"). Then tell them that this project involves a slithery grass dweller—the snake! Provide each child with a 9" x 12" sheet of green construction paper and a copy of the snake patterns on page 45 duplicated onto white construction paper. Invite each youngster to color his snakes as desired, then cut them out. Next demonstrate how to create a weaving mat to represent grass. As students watch and follow along, fold a sheet of green paper in half; then cut slits from the fold toward the edge, being sure to stop about two inches from the edge. Unfold the paper and show youngsters how to weave their cut-out snakes in and out of the slits. Look out—there are snakes in the grass!

Grass-Tasting Gala

Grass is more than the green stuff we find under our feet or a home for creepy "crawlies." The grass family also provides many of the foods we eat every day. Remind students that wheat, corn, oats, barley, rye, rice, and sugarcane are all members of the grass family. Talk about the many different kinds of grasses and the foods they provide, such as cereals, breads, corn, and pasta. Then plan a "Grass-Tasting Gala" with the help of your students' families. Duplicate and send home with each child a copy of the note on page 44. On the designated day, set up a buffet table complete with green paper plates and napkins, and green Easter grass to accent the serving dishes. Then get ready to graze! After the grass tasting, teach little ones the following poem to help reinforce the bounty of grass.

Hula Hoopla

If your youngsters were amazed to find out they *eat* grass, fill them in on other ways that people use grasses. Grasses are used to make furniture, paper, clothing, houses, and even perfume! Invite each of your youngsters to put some artificial grass to good use when she creates a popular grass product—a grass skirt!

Provide each child with a sentence strip and several lengths of green crepe-paper streamer. Have her glue one end of each streamer onto the sentence strip. After the glue has dried, punch a hole at each end of the sentence strip. Thread a length of yarn through each hole and tie it in place. Fit the finished skirt around the child's waist and tie the yarn lengths together. Play a recording of hula music (or any dance music) and invite youngsters to move and groove in their grassy creations!

Grass Can Be Such A Tasty Treat

Grass can be sugar; grass can be wheat;
Grass can be such a tasty treat!
Grass can be barley; grass can be rye;
Taste them! Taste them! Give them a try.
Grass can be corn or grass can be oats;
Try them and you will love them both!
All these are grasses, no matter how they're
    dressed.
And the grass in my tummy is what I like
    best!

Parents—Please Help Us Graze!

On __August 27__, we will be celebrating the wonders of grass with a "Grass-Tasting Gala." We would like each child to bring in one food item to share with the class that day. Please help your child prepare an item from the grass family, such as a food containing corn, oats, sugar, wheat, barley, or rice.

Just put on your thinking caps and go "grazy"! Thanks for your cooperation!

Keep Off The Grass!

This fun variation on the traditional game of Musical Chairs will keep little ones *off* their toes! Begin by asking youngsters if they have ever seen a sign asking that people keep off the grass. Explain that sometimes at a garden or park, a caretaker might want to keep grass from being trampled so that it will look beautiful for everyone to appreciate. Then inform youngsters that keeping off the grass is exactly the object of this game.

Create a circle of chairs to include one less chair than there are children in your group. Inside the circle of chairs, scatter pieces of green crepe-paper streamer to represent grass. Then play some lively music—"Green Grass Grew All Around" from *Greg And Steve: Rocking Down The Road* (Youngheart Music) would be a good choice. Invite little ones to dance on the grass until you stop the music. When the music stops, direct the children to shout, "Keep off the grass!" and quickly find chairs. The child without a seat leaves the circle. Restart the music and remove one chair. Be sure to have a fun activity awaiting the participants who are "out." Perhaps they could begin preparing or eating one of the yummy recipes below.

Grassy Grub

Youngsters will be ready to dig in to either of these great-tasting grass goodies!

Grass Smash

1 cup whipped topping (per child)
1 tablespoon dry instant pistachio pudding mix (per child)
green-tinted coconut

Invite each child to measure one cup of whipped topping and one tablespoon of pudding mix into a zippered plastic bag. Have her "smash" her tightly sealed bag between her hands to mix the ingredients. Help her snip off one corner of the bag and squeeze the mixture into a paper cup. Encourage her to sprinkle a little green-tinted coconut on top before sampling the finished recipe.

Turf Treats

1 ten-ounce package green confectionery coating*
    (found in craft or candy supply stores)
1 three-ounce can chow-mein noodles
Gummy Worms® or bugs

Melt the green candy coating in a microwave or in a double boiler on a portable burner. Let it cool slightly; then stir in the chow-mein noodles until well coated. Drop by tablespoons onto waxed paper and top each Turf Treat with a Gummy Worm® or bug. Refrigerate until the candy is firm.

*If green candy coating is unavailable, try tinting white confectionery coating with oil-based candy coloring (for best results) or regular green food coloring.

Measuring Reproducible

Use with "Grassy 'Guess-timates' " on page 37.

Watch The
Green
Grass
Grow

5

4

3

2

1

Flannelboard Patterns
Use with "The Parts Of The Plant" on page 38.

stem

root bunch

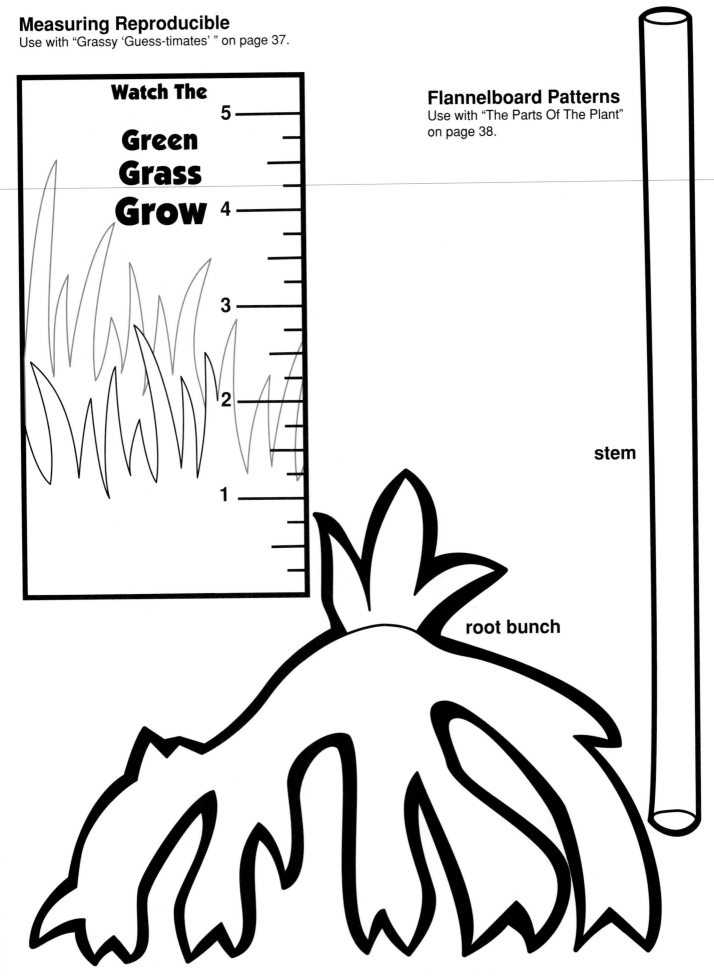

blades

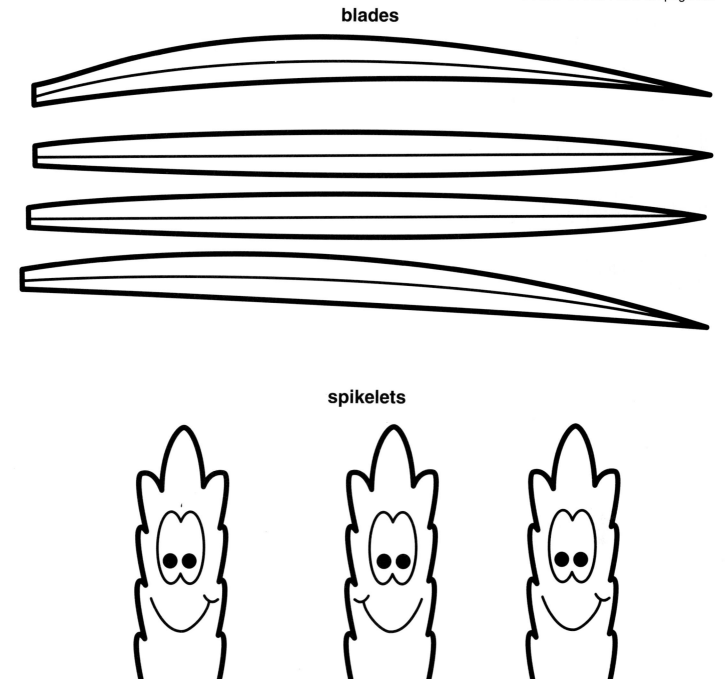

spikelets

Parent Note
Use with "Grass-Tasting Gala" on page 40.

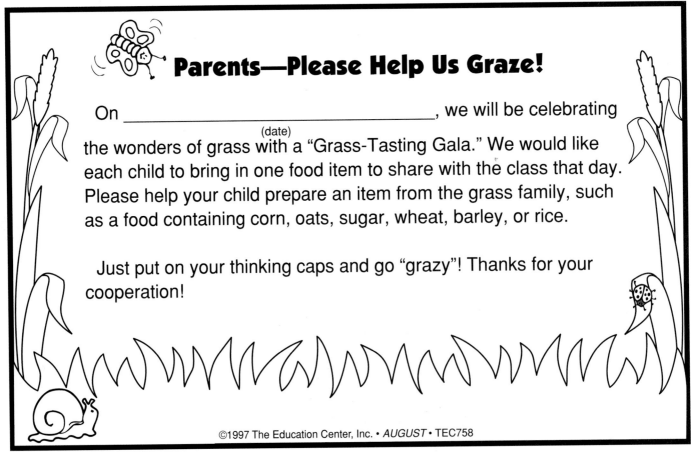

Parents—Please Help Us Graze!

On _____, we will be celebrating
                        (date)
the wonders of grass with a "Grass-Tasting Gala." We would like
each child to bring in one food item to share with the class that day.
Please help your child prepare an item from the grass family, such
as a food containing corn, oats, sugar, wheat, barley, or rice.

   Just put on your thinking caps and go "grazy"! Thanks for your
cooperation!

Parents—Please Help Us Graze!

On _____, we will be celebrating
                        (date)
the wonders of grass with a "Grass-Tasting Gala." We would like
each child to bring in one food item to share with the class that day.
Please help your child prepare an item from the grass family, such
as a food containing corn, oats, sugar, wheat, barley, or rice.

   Just put on your thinking caps and go "grazy"! Thanks for your
cooperation!

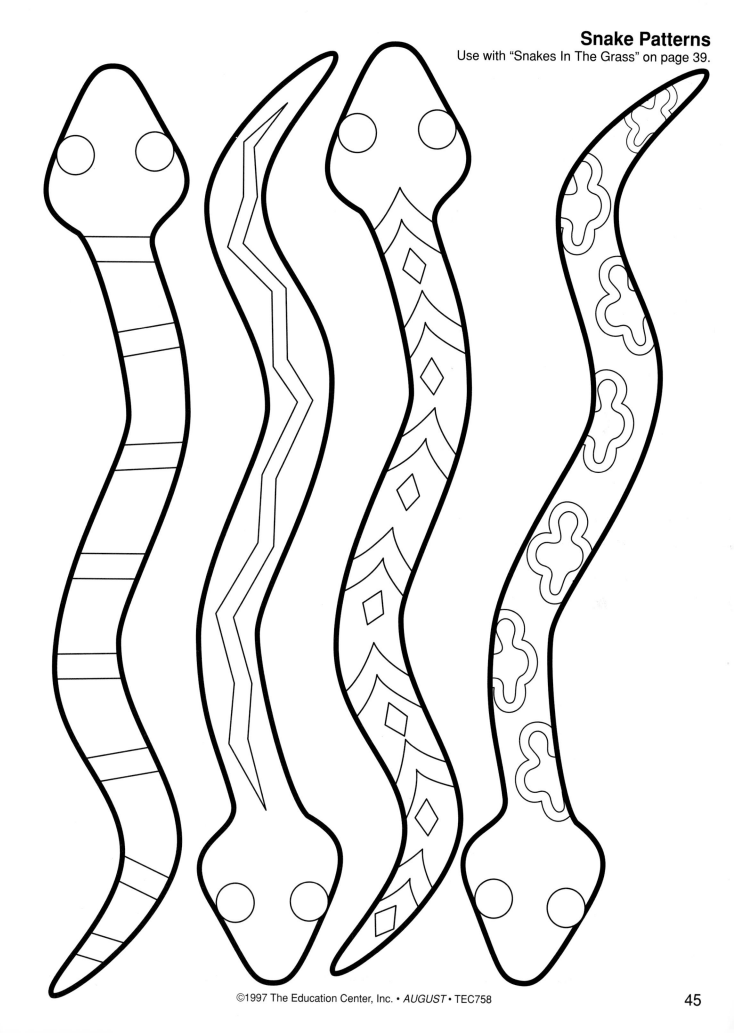

At The Grocery Store

Attention, shoppers! You'll find a cartload of fun, cross-curricular ideas waiting for you when you stroll the aisles of this grocery-store unit.

ideas contributed by Barbara F. Backer

Where Do You Shop?

"Where does your family shop for food?" Begin your grocery-store unit by asking students this very simple question during circle time. Write students' responses on a sheet of chart paper. Then, after everyone has had an opportunity to reply, provide each child with a newspaper containing grocery-store advertisements. Instruct each student to cut out an advertisement that has the name or logo of the store where his family shops. Have each student glue the logo onto the chart next to his name. Tally the results to see which store is the most popular.

What Do We Know?

Get your little ones revved up and ready for a trip to a grocery store with this activity. Invite students to tell you some things they know about the grocery store; then write each child's response on a sheet of chart paper. On another sheet of chart paper, write students' responses to the question, "What do you want to know about the grocery store?"

Create a display for your little ones' grocery-store knowledge by mounting each chart to a bulletin board as shown, leaving enough room for a fourth chart. When you return from your field trip, display a fourth chart titled "What We Learned" (see "To Market, To Market" on page 47). Surround the charts with a border of photos taken during your trip; then top it all off with the heading "To Market, To Market."

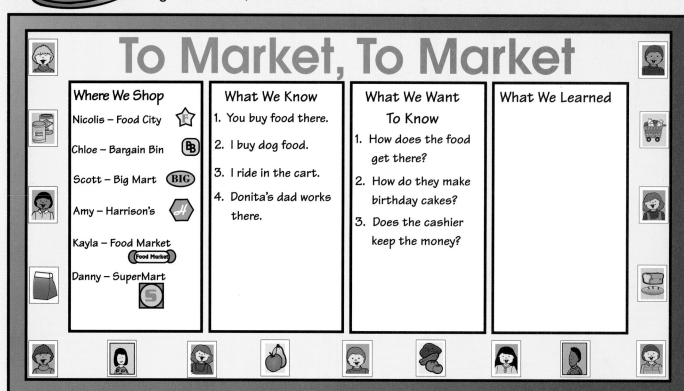

Kimberly Richard

To Market, To Market

The grocery store can be a busy, fascinating place for youngsters! Arrange a field trip to a local grocery store to give students a behind-the-scenes look at the action. In advance contact the store manager to request that your students be given a tour of the store—including such areas as the loading dock and stockrooms. Also advise him of the things students would like to know about the market (refer to the chart made in "What Do We Know?" on page 46).

Before your trip duplicate onto tagboard a nametag (on page 52) for each child. Instruct each child to color, then cut out his nametag. Write his name in the space provided using a black marker. Laminate the nametags; then hot-glue a bar pin (available at craft stores) to the back of each tag. (Save the nametags for later use in "A Store Of Our Own" on page 49.)

During your field trip, point out the numbered overhead signs. Explain to students that each sign tells shoppers which items can be found in that aisle. Conduct a scavenger hunt by asking a student to name a food; then guide a group to find the aisle in which the named food is located.

When you return to the classroom, make a chart of the things your students learned at the grocery store. Hang this chart on the bulletin board created in "What Do We Know?" on page 46.

Bag Of Thanks

Have students express their gratitude to their grocery-store guide with this thank-you note. Duplicate onto construction paper a class supply of the grocery-bag pattern on page 52. Instruct each child to color the food items and cut out her note. Write each child's dictation for her thank-you message on the front of the bag; then have her sign her note. Bind all the pages together between construction-paper covers; then place the resulting book inside a brown paper bag. Deliver the bagged book to the grocery store. Now that's a bagful of heartfelt thanks!

Sing A Song Of Grocery Stores

Follow up your trip to the grocery store with this little ditty that encourages students to recall some things they saw while at the store. After each verse select a different child to name something she saw at the grocery store; then substitute her name and item in the corresponding phrases.

(sung to the tune of "Mary Had A Little Lamb")

(chorus)
We went to the grocery store,
Grocery store, grocery store.
We went to the grocery store,
And this is what we saw.

(verse)
[Shevonne] saw [some ice cream],
[Some ice cream], [some ice cream].
[Shevonne] saw [some ice cream],
When we went to the store.

Sitting in the grocery cart,
I had a lot of fun.

I saw *a birthday cake*

In aisle number 1.

1.

A Cart With A View

Your little ones will love taking home these books to share about their visit to the grocery store. Duplicate the verses on page 53 for each child. To make a book, have a child cut out a set of verses on the bold lines, then glue each verse to the bottom of a sheet of paper. On each page instruct the child to draw a picture of something he saw at the grocery store. Then write the student's completion to the verse on the line provided. (For the purposes of this activity, it won't matter if the food the child names was actually in the aisle specified on each page.) Continue in the same manner until all the pages are complete. Sequence and bind the pages between construction-paper covers. Urge students to take their books home to share with their families.

48

A Store Of Our Own

Once youngsters have had an opportunity to see how a grocery store operates, extend learning opportunities by building a classroom grocery store.

Setting Up And Stocking The Shelves

- Prepare a divided shelf for displaying cans and boxes.
- Send home a note requesting that parents send in clean, empty food packages. Fill boxes with crumpled newspaper to prevent them from collapsing; then seal the ends with clear tape. Use pliers to crimp down sharp edges on food cans. Then—as an added precaution—cover the rims with duct tape.
- Display plastic fruits and vegetables in baskets on a low table or shelf.
- Create a meat display by placing plastic meats from the housekeeping area on sanitized Styrofoam® trays, then wrapping each tray with plastic wrap.
- Set up a check-out lane by covering a table with bulletin-board paper. Create a scanner by making an *X* with masking tape. (Youngsters will love making a "beep" sound each time an item is "scanned"!)
- Place a toy cash register, telephone, pencils, and paper at one end of the table. Fill the cash register with play money.
- Gather a collection of various-size paper bags and place them at the opposite end of the table. (For safety reasons, do not provide plastic bags.)
- Collect a supply of handled baskets for little shoppers.
- Stock the center with some purses and wallets. Fill each with some play money.
- Provide a few aprons and the nametags from "To Market, To Market" (page 47) for your young clerks, cashiers, and stockers.

A Store Full Of Learning Opportunities

Now that you have the basics for your store, set the stage for center success by enlisting the help of your students to complete the following tasks:

- Assist a group of students in stocking the shelves of the store, guiding them to display similar items together.
- Encourage a small group of youngsters to create display signs for the items in the store.
- Take a class poll to decide on a name for the store. Then create a store-front sign and logo to hang in your classroom store.
- Assist students in deciding how many children may play in the store at a time.
- Decide how to restock the shelves after they have been emptied.

Shop And Sing

Create some mood music for your grocery store by teaching your youngsters the song below. When students have learned the words, tape-record them singing. On the same tape, record some other songs about the grocery store—such as "Let's Go To The Market" by Greg and Steve from *We All Live Together: Vol. 5* (Youngheart Music). Invite students to play the tape while they are shopping.

(sung to the tune of "Clementine")

At the grocery store, at the grocery store,
We can buy good things to eat.
Milk and yogurt, bread and cereal,
And bananas—what a treat!

Fresh tomatoes, bright green broccoli,
Fish and meat, or a canned ham.
Tacos, egg rolls, sweet potatoes,
And some food for my dog, Sam.

Put the groceries in the basket,
Walking up and down the aisles.
Get in line to buy your groceries.
When you pay, the grocer smiles.

One-Stop Snack Shopping

Who doesn't enjoy a market that provides samples for its shoppers? Turn snacktime into sample time in your classroom grocery store. Set up a small table; then cover it with a tablecloth. Each day invite a few students to prepare the snack just as they would if they were serving samples in a grocery store. For example, students might place cookies or crackers in individual sandwich bags, or poke toothpicks into fruit or cheese chunks, then serve a few on a small paper plate. Have students choose a snack sample by approaching the table and selecting a sample along with a small paper cup of juice. One bite and your little shoppers will be sold on this idea!

All Sorts Of Groceries

Now that youngsters have had opportunities to play in your classroom grocery store, use the product containers to introduce some sorting and classifying activities. During a group time, ask students to estimate which type of container is most prevalent in your grocery store: plastic containers, boxes, or cans. Write each student's guess on the chalkboard or a sheet of paper. Then collect the containers from the shelves and have students sort them into like groups. Count the number of containers in each group. Did anyone guess correctly?

Extend this activity on another day by providing pairs of students with a grocery bag full of containers. Have each pair sort the contents of its bag into three groups—plastic, cans, and boxes. Then challenge students to find other ways of sorting their items—such as numbers/no numbers, labels/no labels, edible/nonedible, or small/large. With a little prompting, students will find all sorts of ways to sort!

Grocery Dominoes

Students will enjoy practicing matching skills with this grocery-store version of dominoes. Duplicate a copy of the game picture cards on page 54 for each child. To make a set of cards, have each youngster cut apart one sheet of picture cards. Instruct her to glue each picture as shown onto a separate end of a divided note card to create a domino. Stack the completed dominoes together. To play, place one domino faceup in the center of a playing table. Give six dominoes to each player in a small group. Have a student in the group place one end of one of her dominoes next to the matching end of a domino on the table. If she doesn't have a match, instruct her to take a domino from the stack. Play continues until no additional matches can be made.

Grocery-Store Bingo

The shelves won't be empty for long with this version of bingo. Duplicate onto construction paper a bingo card (on page 55) for each child. Also duplicate onto construction paper a class supply—plus one extra—of the game picture cards (on page 54). Instruct each child to cut out a sheet of game cards. Have her select eight pictures, then glue four pictures to each shelf on her bingo card. Make caller cards by gluing each game picture from the extra set to a separate index card. Laminate all the cards for durability if desired.

To play, provide each player with a supply of pennies to use as markers. Have a volunteer randomly select a caller card from a box, then name the picture on the card. If a child has a matching picture on her card, she may cover it with a penny. When a player has covered every picture on her card, she may call out, "The shelves are full!" Continue play until each child has covered all the pictures on her card.

Nametag

Use with "To Market, To Market" on page 47 and "A Store Of Our Own" on page 49.

Thank-You Card

Use with "Bag Of Thanks" on page 47.

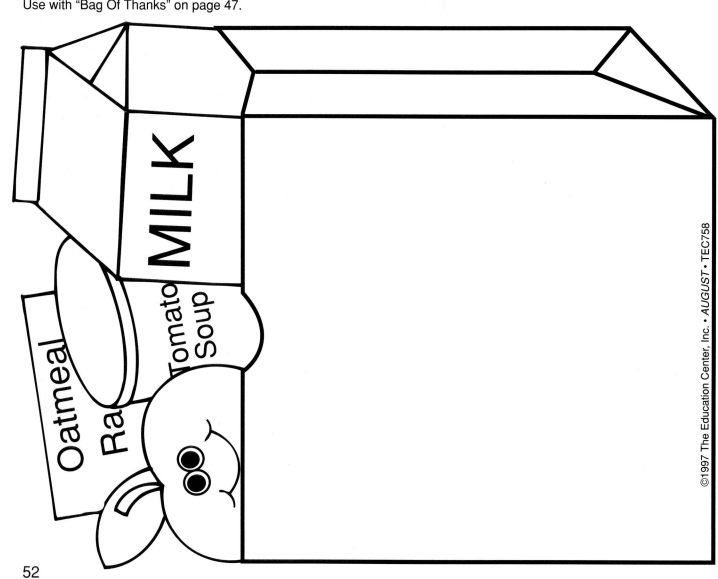

2.

Sitting in the
grocery cart,
You know it's true;

I saw _____

In aisle number **2.**

©1997 The Education Center, Inc. • AUGUST • TEC758

4.

Sitting in the
grocery cart,
Near the front door,

I saw _____

In aisle number **4.**

©1997 The Education Center, Inc. • AUGUST • TEC758

1.

Sitting in the
grocery cart,
I had a lot of fun.

I saw _____

In aisle number **1.**

©1997 The Education Center, Inc. • AUGUST • TEC758

3.

Sitting in the
grocery cart,
Happy as could be,

I saw _____

In aisle number **3.**

©1997 The Education Center, Inc. • AUGUST • TEC758

Game Picture Cards

Use with "Grocery Dominoes" and "Grocery-Store Bingo" on page 51.

Grocery-Store Bingo

Hooray For Hats!

"Cap-italize" on your little ones' fascination with hats when you head into this unit.

ideas contributed by Ada Goren and Lucia Kemp Henry

Why Do We Wear Hats?

Before beginning your unit on hats, gather a wide variety of headgear—such as a baseball cap, a dress-up crown, a snow hat, a sun hat, a football or bicycle helmet, career hats from your dramatic-play area, and any hats from other cultures that you might have. Seat youngsters in a circle and pass the hats around for everyone to see and touch. Then pose the question, "Why do we wear hats?" As children examine the hats, they'll no doubt come up with several reasons. Guide them to realize that hats can be used as protection for the head, as part of a uniform, or just for looking good!

Follow up your discussion by reading aloud the photo-illustrated book *Hats, Hats, Hats* by Ann Morris (Mulberry Books). Then ask youngsters to list as many different types of hats as they can, using your hat examples and the pictures in the book to get them started. Write the list on a sheet of chart paper and post it on a classroom wall.

A Musical Follow-Up

After discussing the many different kinds of hats, try this activity to build children's vocabulary and review the purposes of various hats. Set out the variety of hats you gathered for "Why Do We Wear Hats?" Then teach youngsters the song below. Repeat the verse as many times as desired, each time substituting a different descriptive phrase in the third line. At the end of each verse, ask a student volunteer to choose a hat from your collection that fits the description. Ask him to name the hat and elaborate on who might wear the hat or for what purpose it might be worn.

Oh Where, Oh Where, Can My Favorite Hat Be?
(sung to the tune of "Oh Where, Oh Where Has My Little Dog Gone?")

Oh where, oh where, can my favorite hat be?
Oh where, oh where can it be?
It's just right for [a hot, sunny day]
Oh where, oh where can it be?

Hats Here, Hats There, Hats In Centers Everywhere!

Hats For Dramatic Play

Of course hats make quick-and-easy costumes for dramatic play every day. But really dress up your dramatic-play area for this unit by transforming it into a hat shop! Shop garage sales and ask parents to donate old hats of all types until you have a large collection of sports hats, fashion hats, and dress-up hats (such as crowns, pirate hats, or cowboy hats). Display the hats in your dramatic-play center on tabletops, hat racks, or even a sheet of Peg-a-Board fitted with cup hooks. Provide several mirrors, a toy cash register, and play money, too. Add old scarves and silk flowers for accessorizing hats. Then invite little ones to try this center on for size!

Hats Off To Math!

A collection of baseball caps will add numeral-sequencing practice to your math center. In advance collect ten old baseball caps (from yard sales, thrift shops, or parent donations). Cut large numerals—1 through 10—from paper or felt. Staple or tape one numeral to the crown of each cap as shown. Then string a clothesline between two chairs in your math center and add some clothespins to the line. Place the caps in a small laundry basket; then challenge each youngster who visits the center to clip the caps to the clothesline in numerical order.

Hat Matching

This matching game will provide individual practice with visual discrimination. Visit your local craft store and purchase an even number of miniature straw hats (available for less than $1.00 each). Then use rickrack, ribbon scraps, tiny silk flowers, or whatever craft materials you have on hand to decorate the hats in matching pairs. Next cut tagboard rectangles to size, so that two hats fit neatly on each rectangle. Glue one hat from a pair on each card. Store the remaining hats in a basket or—better yet—a hatbox. To use this center, a child chooses a card, then finds the matching hat to place on the open space on the card. Encourage him to continue until he's matched all the hats.

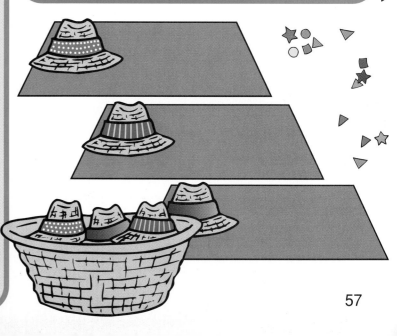

Hats In The Art Center

Provide the materials for students to complete one, two, or all three of the following hat projects in your art center.

Fancy Fantasy Hats

Put your little designers to work creating fantasy hats just brimming with imagination! First duplicate page 60 on white construction paper for each child. Also cut an assortment of large, colored construction-paper shapes and set out a variety of craft materials—such as buttons, feathers, ribbon, pipe cleaners, and crinkled gift-wrap stuffing. When a child visits the center, ask him to use crayons to make the face on his pattern resemble himself. Instruct each child to choose a few colored shapes to create the basic shape of his hat, then glue them in place. Invite him to use the craft materials of his choice to embellish his hat design. When his masterpiece is complete, fill in his dictated description of his hat on the blank line.

My fancy hat is COOL!

1.
2.
3.
4.

Classic Newspaper Hats

These are always fun to wear, but they'll also be fun for little ones to decorate! In advance fold a newspaper hat for each child, following the steps shown above. Or, to develop a youngster's fine-motor skills and ability to follow directions, ask a child to follow along as you demonstrate how to fold a hat. Then set out shaped sponges, shallow trays of tempera paint in a variety of colors, and an assortment of trims, such as feathers, ribbon, pom-pom braid, or rickrack. Invite each child to sponge-paint designs on the top (triangular) part of his hat, then glue the trim of his choice along the brim. Allow the paint and glue to dry before having youngsters try on their hats.

Paper-Bag Hats

Stock your art center with medium-size brown grocery bags, die-cut construction-paper shapes, glue, and markers or paint pens. When a child visits the center, assist her in folding down the open edge of a bag several times to create a rolled hat brim. Staple the brim in place; then encourage the child to color or glue the designs of her choice on the bag. What a charming chapeau!

Show Off Your Chapeaus!

Of course youngsters will be anxious to show off their works of millinery art! Plan a simple parade around your school or center, with each child wearing a hat of her own design. If desired mount each child's design from "Fancy Fantasy Hats" on a hallway bulletin board or around your door to inform visitors of the theme in progress.

Hat Books Are Tops

If you enhance your learning centers with the ideas on pages 57 and 58, you'll also want to enhance storytime with these books featuring hats.

Whose Hat?
Written by Margaret Miller
Published by Mulberry Books

The very simple text and photos in this book focusing on hats for various careers are especially appealing for preschoolers. After sharing the book, create an innovation that will help little ones recognize classmates' names and faces at the beginning of the year. Invite each child to bring a hat of her choice from home. With an instant camera and plenty of film on hand, take a photo of each individual hat (lying on a table-top), then of each child wearing her hat. Sequence the photos on bound half-sheets of construction paper, with the words "Whose hat?" on a left-hand page and a photo of a hat on a right-hand page. Flip the page, write "[Child's name]'s hat!" on the left, and attach the photo of the child wearing that same hat on the right-hand page. Your little ones will delight in identifying their friends as they "read" this class book again and again!

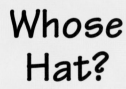

Whose Hat?

Jennie's Hat
Written by Ezra Jack Keats
Published by HarperCollins Children's Books

Read aloud this classic story about a girl whose hat is too plain for her liking. Point out the part of the story in which Jennie tries on a variety of household objects in search of a suitable hat. Then ask youngsters to look around your classroom for items that could be worn as hats. Invite each child to bring an item to the circle. Then have a "Not-A-Hat" fashion show, encouraging each child to model her makeshift headgear for the group.

Follow up your fashion show with the perfect refreshments—hat-shaped snacks! Give each child a large sugar cookie, a marshmallow, a pretzel stick, and some peanut butter. Have her use peanut butter to stick the marshmallow to the center of the cookie. Then provide an assortment of sprinkles and invite each youngster to use bits of peanut butter (applied with her pretzel stick) to "glue" sprinkle decorations to her hat. Your little ones can embellish their edible hats until they're just as fancy as Jennie's hat at the end of the story!

More Topper Tales

A Hat So Simple
Written by Jerry Smath
Published by BridgeWater Books

Juice The Pig
Written by Martine Oborne
Published by Henry Holt And Company, Inc.

A Hat For Minerva Louise
Written by Janet Morgan Stoeke
Published by Puffin Books

Who Took The Farmer's Hat?
Written by Joan L. Nôdset
Published by HarperCollins Children's Books

A Three Hat Day
Written by Laura Geringer
Published by HarperCollins Children's Books

This Is The Hat
Written by Nancy Van Laan
Published by Hyperion Books For Children

My fancy hat is

Note To The Teacher: Use with "Fancy Fantasy Hats" on page 58.

Cookies, Crackers, Math, & Me

Get ready to crunch and munch your way into math skills with those incredible edibles—cookies and crackers! Help little ones develop skills with shapes, patterning, counting, measurement, graphing, and numeral recognition with these activities that are good enough to eat.

ideas contributed by Ada Goren and Suzanne Moore

Cracker Matchers

Crackers come in so many shapes and sizes, they're the perfect tool for reinforcing matching skills. To prepare for this activity (and for "Shape Up With Crackers"), purchase—or ask parents to donate—several types of crackers in different shapes and sizes. For each child, prepare a zippered plastic bag containing five matching pairs of crackers, ten in all. Distribute a bag of crackers and a paper towel to each child. Ask each youngster to empty her bag and match the pairs of crackers atop her paper towel. When all the matches have been made, ask a volunteer to tell how she found each match. Lead children to understand that they used their sense of sight to determine the likenesses of their crackers in shape and size. Then make the matching a bit more challenging.

Give each child a second paper towel. Ask her to remove one cracker from each pair and replace it in the plastic bag, leaving the bag lying flat on the tabletop. Then have her cover the bag with the second paper towel. Have her identify one of the crackers still showing, then reach into the covered bag and attempt to find the matching cracker using only her sense of touch. Of course, little ones will want to munch their matches when they're all through! Wouldn't you?

Shape Up With Crackers

Move from matching to identifying shapes with this delicious rhyme. For each child, place a few differently shaped crackers into a zippered plastic bag. You'll also need a set of attribute blocks (or poster-board cutouts) in corresponding shapes. Place these in their own plastic bag. To begin, give each child a bag of crackers. Then pull one attribute block or poster-board shape from the bag, and have students identify its shape. Then have youngsters recite the following rhyme as each child looks for that shape of cracker in his bag. If he has a cracker of that shape, he may crunch into it before the next shape is pulled.

Mmmmm!
Crackers, crackers, what a treat!
[Shape] crackers are good to eat!
Mmmmm!

61

Pam Crane

Snack-Mix Measurement

Serve up a class-size portion of introductory measurement skills with this activity. In advance, purchase—or ask parents to donate—the ingredients listed in the snack-mix recipe. Bring in a measuring cup and ask little ones to help you measure and mix this tasty treat. First model proper measurement techniques, pointing out the lines on your measuring cup and showing students how to fill a cup to its exact volume. Then encourage student volunteers to try their hands at measuring the recipe ingredients into a big bowl. Give every child a turn to stir the mixture with a large wooden spoon. Then, working with one small group at a time, have each child carefully measure a half-cup serving onto a paper plate. Before having them munch the mix, have students sort and graph the ingredients (see "Egg-Carton Graphs").

Egg-Carton Graphs

These lightweight, compartmentalized containers are perfect for making real graphs with small items—including small cookies and crackers. To make one, cut the lids from two egg cartons. Connect the bases with brads. You now have a four-column graph! Need more columns? Just add another egg-carton base or two!

To sort and graph the ingredients from "Snack-Mix Measurement," supply each child in a small group with an egg-carton graph. Have her sort the four ingredients into the four columns on her graph, then compare her results. Use this opportunity to introduce the mathematical terms *most, fewest,* and *equal.*

Crunchy-Munchy Mix
(makes 16 half-cup servings)

2 cups Ritz® Bits® minicrackers
2 cups Goldfish® crackers
2 cups miniature pretzels
2 cups cinnamon-graham stars

To Twist Or Not To Twist?

Mmmm...sandwich cookies! Some folks just take a big bite, while others twist off one cookie layer and eat the filling first. To find out which way each of your students prefers to eat a sandwich cookie, prepare a two-column graph on a large piece of bulletin-board paper. At the top of one column, glue a construction-paper cookie with a "bite" taken out of it. At the top of the other column, show two construction-paper circles—one with cotton glued onto it to resemble cookie filling.

Ask each child to write his name on a sticky note and place the note in the column illustrating his preferred cookie-eating method. Then pass out sandwich cookies and have little ones demonstrate their preferences firsthand! After the treat, discuss the results of the graph. Extend this activity on another day by graphing whether little ones prefer to dunk their cookies in milk before eating them.

"Chocolate Chip, Peanut Butter, Chocolate Chip, Peanut Butter..."

Cookies make for some palatable patterning practice! In advance, ask parents to send in an assortment of cookies. Working with one small group at a time, have students wash their hands before beginning this activity. Spread a supply of cookies on a table; then demonstrate a simple pattern involving two types of cookies, such as *chocolate chip, peanut butter, chocolate chip, peanut butter.* Ask a volunteer to extend your pattern, using the cookies on the table. Repeat this exercise a few times, using different types of cookies. Then ask students to work together in pairs. Encourage one child to create a simple two-cookie pattern; then ask his partner to extend it.

More advanced youngsters may be ready for more difficult patterns, involving varying repetitions or a greater number of cookies. However far your patterning practice takes you, end the activity by asking each child in the group to select one cookie from those remaining in the packages. Then challenge the children to arrange themselves in a pattern before inviting them to eat their cookies.

To Twist Or Not To Twist?

⬤⭕	◖
Juan	Todd
Katie	Kyle
Dallas	Allie
Cara	

Cookie Questions

Conduct a survey—and a little counting practice—to find out the favorite cookies of your youngsters' families and friends. First duplicate the cookie survey sheet on page 65 for each child. Tell little ones to take the sheet home and ask each family member (or any friends they'd like to have participate) to indicate her favorite type of cookie by drawing a happy face in a square beside it. Instruct students to have their parents assist them in counting the number of happy faces beside each type of cookie and in writing the corresponding numeral in the column marked "Total." Have your young pollsters return the survey sheets on the designated day. If desired, count the total number of people in your extended classroom family who prefer each type of cookie and determine an overall favorite.

Cookie Questionnaire
Draw a happy face beside the type of cookie you like best.

Name	Mom	Dad	Granny	Carrie	Timmy		Total
chocolate chip	☺		☺	☺			3
peanut butter		☺					1
sugar					☺		1
oatmeal							

Name _Carrie_

Please return this survey sheet to school on ___8/19___

"Nummy" Number Cookies

There's no more delicious way to reinforce numeral recognition than to make number cookies. To prepare for this activity, check your local craft or discount store to find a set of numeral-shaped cookie cutters. Then purchase a few rolls of refrigerated sugar-cookie dough or prepare your favorite recipe in quantity.

Divide your class into small groups and have each group work with an adult. Have everyone wash her hands before beginning. Invite young-sters to help roll out the sugar-cookie dough on a floured surface. Then have each child press a numeral-shaped cutter into the dough. Ask her to place the unbaked cookie on a baking sheet and identify the numeral. To add practice with creating sets, provide M&M's®, raisins, or chocolate chips. Have each child count out the corresponding number of cookie decorations to press onto her unbaked cookie. Invite children to continue taking turns making cookies until your dough is depleted. Then bake the cookies according to package or recipe directions.

Invite a neighboring class to help you nibble your number cookies, or send each school helper a small plastic bag containing a few cookies and a note that reads, "We *number* you among our best friends!"

Cookie Questionnaire

Draw a happy face beside the type of cookie you like best.

Name							Total
chocolate chip							
peanut butter							
sugar							
oatmeal							

Name _____

Please return this survey sheet to school on _____.

(date)

©1997 The Education Center, Inc. • AUGUST • TEC758

Note To The Teacher: Use with "Cookie Questions" on page 64.

65

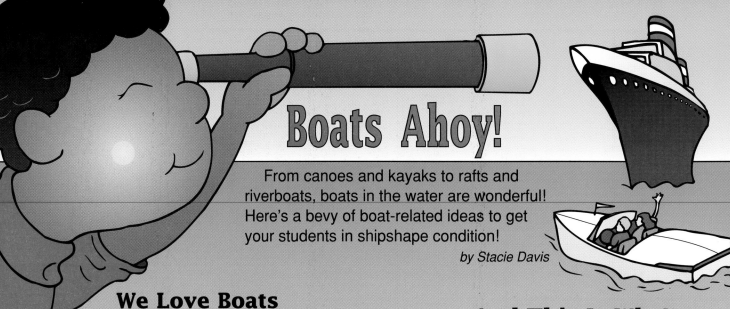

Boats Ahoy!

From canoes and kayaks to rafts and riverboats, boats in the water are wonderful! Here's a bevy of boat-related ideas to get your students in shipshape condition!

by Stacie Davis

We Love Boats

Launch your boat unit with a reading of Flora McDonnell's book *I Love Boats* (Candlewick Press). With its simple text and bold illustrations, this book is bound to delight your youngsters. Before sharing the book, print the following poem on a sheet of chart paper and post it near your circle area. After reading the book, share the poem with your students.

[Big] boats,
[Little] boats,
Any kind of boats.
I love boats!

[Fast] boats,
[Slow] boats,
Any kind of boats.
I love boats!

Boats that [sail],
Boats that [race],
Any kind of boats.
I love boats!

Boats in the [ocean],
Boats in the [lake],
Any kind of boats.
I love boats!

Repeat the poem as many times as desired, inviting students to replace the underlined words with other adjectives, verbs, and bodies of water.

...And This Is Why!

As a follow-up to the activity at left, invite students to tell you why *they* love boats. Provide each student with a construction-paper boat cutout. Ask her to dictate what she thinks about boats as you write her comment on her cutout. Display the cutout comments on and around your classroom doorway with the title "We Love Boats!" to let everyone know about your boat study.

I like boats because they go fast.

I like boats because they have pretty sails.

A Bevy Of Boats

Help your students recognize that there are many different kinds of boats. Begin by sharing *Boat Book* by Gail Gibbons (Holiday House, Inc.). Afterward guide students to understand that many of the boats featured in the book perform specific functions or tasks, while other boats are used for pleasure. Then challenge students to recall the names of pictured boats and their primary use: for work or for fun. List students' responses on a chart as shown.

Boats for work	Boats for fun
fireboat police boat submarine tugboat freighter	canoe sailboat cabin cruiser fishing boat kayak

Big-City Port

The book *Big City Port* by Betsy Maestro and Ellen DelVecchio (Four Winds Press) is another excellent book to share with students to help them learn boat names. After reading this book, have students make their own bustling big-city port with this cooperative project. First create a harbor by filling a shallow container with water and setting it atop a table. Provide an assortment of materials—such as milk containers, film canisters, craft sticks, foam trays, and cereal boxes—so children can create buildings and piers to place around the harbor. Provide some toy boats (or invite children to bring toy boats from home) to set sail in the harbor.

Name That Boat

Your first-rate mates will enjoy this tune about different kinds of working boats. To prepare the flannelboard figures for this activity, duplicate page 74 for future use; then mount the boat patterns on page 73 on tagboard. Cut out and laminate each pattern for durability. Attach the hook side of a piece of Velcro® to the back of each cutout. As the class sings each verse, have a different student affix the boat mentioned to the flannelboard.

The Working Boat Song
(sung to the tune of "Mary Had A Little Lamb")

Here's a little tugboat.
It will push; it will pull.
This boat helps to move a barge
When it is really full.

Here's a helpful fishing boat,
Used in sun; used in sleet.
People on this fishing boat
Catch food for us to eat.

Here's a great big ferryboat.
Drive right on in your car!
This very nifty ferryboat
Will take you near and far.

Here's a special fireboat.
See a fire? Give a shout!
This hardworking fireboat
Will help to put it out!

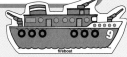

Cruising With Class

Cruise into nautical fun with this nifty idea! In advance transform your classroom into the deck of a cruise ship. To do this, push aside your tables and chairs to create an open floor space. Position beach chairs around your room. Set a large beach umbrella on the floor with beach towels scattered beneath it. Use masking tape to mark off a modified shuffleboard court on the floor. Have a pitcher of ice-cold fruit juice ready to serve your parched passengers. Then, as students arrive—donning sunglasses and straw hats they've brought from home—greet them with a hearty hello. Have an instant camera handy so you can snap a head-and-shoulders photo of each of your little passengers. (Save the photos for later use.)

Begin the day's lessons by surveying students to determine if anyone has ever been on a real cruise ship. If desired, invite a travel agent to your classroom to show students cruise-ship posters and brochures. Then engage in a few modified games of shuffleboard by simply inviting youngsters to use brooms to gently push inverted plastic bowls into the playing court. Continue the cruise with a little pleasure reading on the deck, and—of course—a seagoing snack. Guide students to understand that cruise ships are not used for work, but as a means to having fun. Bon voyage!

Who's That Peeping From The Porthole?

Before students disembark from your cruise ship, engage them in this fun project that results in a classy bulletin board. Prepare for this activity by duplicating a white construction-paper copy of the cruise-ship pattern on page 72 for each student. Using an X-acto® knife, carefully cut out each porthole as indicated. Also cut a class supply of white construction-paper speech bubbles. Then give each student a cruise-ship pattern to color and cut out. Help each student tape his photo behind the porthole cutout so that his face is visible. Afterward enlist students' help in naming things that one could see while traveling on a cruise ship. Then ask each student, "[Child's name], [Child's name], what do you see?" Invite each student to complete the sentence "I see a [name of item] looking at me." Print both sentences—along with each student's dictation—on a speech bubble. Staple each child's boat and speech bubble onto a bulletin board that has been covered with blue construction paper and titled "Classy Cruisers."

Sail Away

Share Donald Crews's delightful book *Sail Away* (Greenwillow Books) with your students. After reading the book, sail into some fine-motor fun. Give each child a sheet of light blue construction paper on which you've drawn a wave design as shown. Have each child carefully cut on the line, providing help as needed. Then give each student a half sheet of construction paper and a supply of colorful, precut, construction-paper shapes. Have him arrange the shapes atop the construction paper to create a small sailboat; then assist each student in gluing his shapes onto the construction paper. After the glue is dry, cut around the boat shape; then help each child tape his project to a craft stick. Show him how to insert the stick into the construction-paper ocean to "sail" the boat. While children are sailing their boats, sing the "Sail Your Boat" song aloud. If desired give each student a copy of the song to glue to his construction-paper ocean. Sail away!

Sail Your Boat
(sung to the tune of "Row, Row, Row Your Boat")

Sail, sail, sail your boat,
On the ocean blue.
Merrily, merrily, merrily, merrily,
Boats are great, it's true!

Colorful Boats

Chart the course for learning with this colorful bookmaking activity. Duplicate one copy of the booklet (on pages 74 and 75) for each student. To make a booklet, cut around the bold outlines on each of the duplicated pages. Glue the four booklet pages together to make one long strip, using the symbols for assistance. Afterward read the text together and have each youngster use the appropriate colors to illustrate a simple sailboat on each page. Then help each student accordion-fold his booklet and add his name to the cover. Encourage students to take their booklets home to read to family members.

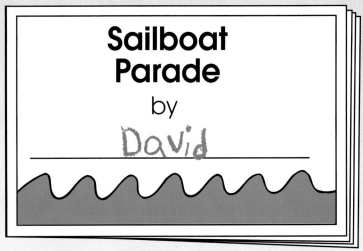

The Real Thing

Your students have read about boats, sung about boats, illustrated boats, and even ventured out on a classroom cruise. Now it's time to take a look at some *real* boats! If you live near a river, a lake, or an ocean, you might arrange a field trip to a harbor, a marina, or a boat dock so that little ones can get a closer look at many different kinds and sizes of boats. You might even arrange a boat ride! Take along lots of adult helpers to provide the close supervision necessary for such a trip.

Create these adorable nametags to set the mood for your field trip. Purchase rolls of wood-grain and patterned Con-Tact® paper. (You might use a different colorful design for each chaperone's group.) For each child, cut a semicircle (approximately four inches on the straight edge) and a 4" x 1/2" strip from the wood-grain paper, as well as a 3" x 3" x 4 1/2" triangle from the patterned Con-Tact® paper. Peel away just enough of the backing on the strip to attach it to the semicircle—as shown—to create a mast. Then peel away enough of the backing on one three-inch side of the triangle to attach it to the wood-grain strip, so that it resembles a sail. Program each nametag with a child's name. On field-trip day, simply peel away the remaining backing and stick each child's nametag to her clothing.

Let's Make Our Own!

After learning about many different kinds of boats, youngsters will want to create some water-worthy vessels of their own. Before diving into boat-making, challenge youngsters to perform a science experiment to determine the best materials to use. Begin by gathering a wide variety of craft materials—such as Styrofoam® meat trays, craft foam, margarine tubs, milk cartons, cereal boxes, sponges, modeling clay, paper plates, craft felt, and construction paper. Place these items on a table near your water table. Then prepare a chart as shown, with a simple picture and label for each material. (Photograph each material, if desired, and tape the pictures to the chart.) Invite youngsters to visit the water table, test the items shown, and mark an "S" (for sink) or an "F" (for float) below each material pictured.

After a day or two of experimenting, discuss the results of the chart and have little ones determine the best boat-making materials. Then let the boatbuilding begin! Provide scissors as well as waterproof glue and modeling clay for holding together boat parts. After youngsters fashion their vessels, allow time for water testing each boat in your water table or a wading pool set up in your outdoor play area.

Will it sink? Or will it float? Is it good to make a boat?

paper plate	milk carton	meat tray	margarine tub	sponge	paper
S	F F	F F	F	F	S

Citrus Sailers

These tantalizing treats are sure to be a hit with your little navigators. To make a treat, provide each child with an orange wedge placed atop a small paper plate. Then give each student a triangular slice of orange and a coffee stirring stick. Assist each student in skewering his orange-slice sail onto the stirring-stick mast. Gently push the resulting sail into the orange-wedge boat. Eat and enjoy!

Banana Barges

Make a bevy of banana barges for a midmorning snack. To make a barge, give each student a banana that has been cut in half lengthwise. Working atop a paper plate, help each student spread a small amount of peanut butter on the cut side of her banana. Provide each student with six to eight raisins to sprinkle over the peanut butter to resemble containers of cargo. Invite students to eat their snacks while you read aloud a book from the literature list on this page.

Shipshape Stories

Boats
Written by Anne Rockwell
Published by E. P. Dutton

Harbor
Written by Donald Crews
Published by Greenwillow Books

The Boats On The River
Written by Marjorie Flack
Published by Troll Associates

Boats
Written by Ken Robbins
Published by Scholastic Inc.

My Blue Boat
Written by Chris L. Demarest
Published by Harcourt Brace & Company

Four Brave Sailors
Written by Mirra Ginsburg
Published by Greenwillow Books

Cruise-Ship Pattern

Use with "Who's That Peeping From The Porthole?" on page 68.

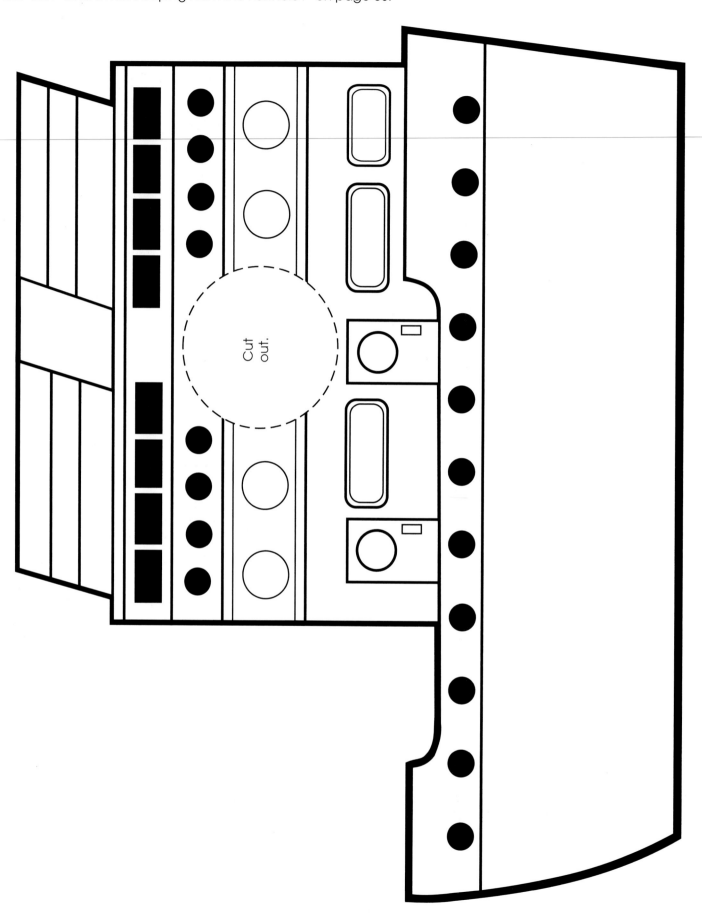

Cut out.

fishing boat

tugboat

ferry

fireboat

Booklet Cover And Pages

Use with "Colorful Boats" on page 69.

Glue * here.

Glue ○ here.

Red boat,

orange boat,

Sailboat Parade

by

yellow boat,

©1997 The Education Center, Inc. • *AUGUST* • TEC758

*

Glue # here.

Green boat,

and a purple boat, too!

and blue.

brown boat,

Let The Teddy Bear Games Begin!

Even though the Olympic® Games come around only once every four years, the Teddy Bear Games are sure to become an annual event in your classroom! Encourage your little ones to strengthen language, math, and motor skills with these "beary" fun activities.

ideas contributed by Vicki Mockaitis Pacchetti

The Main Event

Set the stage for Olympic®-sized excitement by preparing your classroom for your Teddy Bear Games. Make a Teddy Bear Games display to adorn the doorway of your classroom. First paint five paper plates, one in each of the following colors: red, yellow, black, green, and blue. Then duplicate, color, and cut out five copies of the teddy-bear pattern on page 81. Glue one cutout to the center of each plate. Display the plates on your classroom door as shown. Top it off with a banner that reads "Welcome To The Teddy Bear Games!"

Welcome To The Teddy Bear Games!

Bring In The Bears

Now that your room is ready to host the Teddy Bear Games, send out an invitation to the star athletes—students' teddy bears! Duplicate a copy of the bear invitation on page 82 for each child. Invite each child to tell you the name of his bear; then write his response on the line provided. Next ask him to write his name at the bottom of the letter, then place the invitation in an envelope for the child to take home.

When the bears arrive at school, have each child prepare a nametag for his bear. First reduce the teddy-bear pattern (page 81) to the desired size; then duplicate it onto white construction paper. Assist each child in writing his bear's name on the cutout before he colors it and cuts it out. Punch a hole in the top of the cutout; then lace a length of yarn through the hole to create a necklace. Place the necklace around the bear's neck. Have each child carry his bear while participating in "Opening Ceremonies" (page 77).

Benjamen

Dear Benjamen Bear
I really need your help. The Teddy Bear Games are about to start at my school. All of the boys and girls are bringing their bears. We are going to have lots of fun playing games all week long. I can't do it without you.

Opening Ceremonies

Begin the Teddy Bear Games each day by leading youngsters in a rousing round of "Teddy Bear Games Theme Song." Youngsters will delight in marching with their bears in preparation for the day's events.

Teddy Bear Games Theme Song
(sung to the tune of "The Bear Went Over The Mountain")

Let the Teddy Bear Games begin,
Let the Teddy Bear Games begin,
Let the Teddy Bear Games begin,
We'll all share lots of grins.

So let's all have some fun,
And play with everyone.

Oh, the teddy bears are here,
Let's give a great big cheer!
Let's shout it loud and clear—
Enjoy the games this year!

Pass, Please

Your little ones will feel like VIPs when they present these special passes to the Teddy Bear Games. Duplicate and cut out a class supply of the pass card on page 81. For each child, glue a pass to a 5" x 8" piece of tagboard; then program the card with a child's name. Store all the passes in a convenient location in your classroom, or ask each child to keep his pass handy in his cubby. Have students present their passes during each day's events. When a child and his bear friend finish an event, place a teddy-bear stamp or sticker in the appropriate box on his pass.

Teddy Bear Games Gazette

Extra! Extra! Read all about it! Keep parents and others informed of each day's events by posting a daily newsletter. Duplicate several copies of the newsletter on page 84. After each day's events, gather students in a group area to discuss the highlights. Write student comments in the spaces provided on the newsletter form. Then invite a student to illustrate the text. Post the newsletter on your classroom door under the display featured in "The Main Event" (see page 76).

77

Where's My Teddy?

The Events

Once youngsters and their bears are prepared, it's time to start the games! Use the ideas on these two pages to build your young athletes' skills with language, listening, motor development, math, and more.

Reading Marathon

Set the pace for your Teddy Bear Games with a reading marathon. To begin, gather a collection of teddy-bear books (see the list below for some titles). Next prepare a bulletin board with the title "Teddy Bear Book Marathon." Then duplicate and cut out a quantity of the teddy-bear pattern on page 81.

Conduct the marathon by recording how many books from the collection you read aloud to your students during the course of the Teddy Bear Games. After reading a book, display a bear cutout on the bulletin board. Program a strip of construction paper with the name of the book; then attach it to the bear cutout so that it resembles a sweatband. Several times during the Teddy Bear Games, stop to count the number of books read. Now that's an event that really goes the distance!

Teddy Bear, Teddy Bear: A Classic Action Rhyme
Illustrated by Michael Hague
Published by Morrow Junior Books

Alphabears: An ABC Book
Written by Kathleen Hague
Published by Henry Holt And Company, Inc.

Where Does The Brown Bear Go?
Written by Nicki Weiss
Published by Greenwillow Books

Somebody And The Three Blairs
Written by Marilyn Tolhurst
Published by Orchard Books

Where's My Teddy?
Written by Jez Alborough
Published by Candlewick Press

Corduroy
Written by Don Freeman
Published by Puffin Books

Bouncing Bears

Here's a game that will leave your young athletes and their bears bouncing with delight! Spread a sheet on the floor of your classroom; then invite youngsters to gather around the sheet and place their bears on it. Direct each child to hold the edge of the sheet with both hands—lifting and lowering it slowly at first, then faster to make the bears bounce. Have the children continue to bounce the bears for one minute. After a minute, have them lower the sheet back to the floor; then count how many bears bounced off. Place the bears back on the sheet and begin the bounce again.

Musical Bears

Everyone's a winner with this terrific teddy version of Musical Chairs. Assist students in arranging their chairs in a circle. Have each youngster sit on a chair and hold his bear. Ask a volunteer to have his bear "watch" the game, so that there is one less bear than children. Direct students to pass the bears around the circle as you play some fun teddy-bear songs. Periodically stop the music. When the music stops, ask the student with empty hands to choose one bear from the circle to join him at a table. Provide him with a treat bag full of Gummy bears or Teddy Grahams® to snack on while the game continues. Continue play in the same manner until there is one child left holding a bear. Then present that child with a treat bag and enjoy listening to your teddy-bear recordings *without* stopping the music!

Edible Emblem

Ingredients For One:
5 vanilla wafers
colored frosting
5 Gummy bears

Utensils For One:
1 small paper plate
1 plastic knife

Teacher Preparation:
Use food coloring to tint separate bowls of white frosting blue, green, red, yellow, and black.

Edible Emblems

Challenge your little athletes to follow directions when preparing this tasty treat. Gather the necessary ingredients, utensils, and supplies. Duplicate page 84 for later use; then remove page 83 and glue it to a sheet of tagboard. Laminate it for durability, if desired; then cut apart the cards. Invite each child to follow the steps on the recipe cards to prepare an Edible Emblem.

Teddy Estimates

Provide estimation training for your young athletes with this activity. Place a quantity of two colors of teddy-bear counters in a jar. Prepare a floor graph by duplicating the teddy-bear pattern (page 81) onto the same colors of construction paper as the bears in the jar. Cut out the patterns; then place each cutout on the floor as a column heading for a graph. Encourage each student to look at the bears in the jar, then use his estimating skills to predict which color bear is most plentiful. Instruct him to place his stuffed teddy bear under the colored-bear cutout that matches his prediction. When each child has had an opportunity to estimate, count each color of bear counter in the jar. Compare the results to the estimations represented on the graph. Did anyone guess correctly?

Busy Bear Relay

Youngsters will be busy trying to keep their bears in tow as they go the distance in this relay game. Divide your class into teams of four or five students each. Provide each team with a teddy bear. Line up the teams along a starting line; then place cones some distance away, so that one cone is opposite each team. To play give a signal, such as a whistle blow. Upon hearing the signal, the first player on each team takes the bear and runs to his team's cone, around the cone, and then back to the starting line. He passes the bear to the next person, then sits down at the end of the line. Continue play in the same manner until all the members of each team have had a turn and are sitting. Then conduct the race again, changing the motor skill to skipping, hopping, or jumping.

Closing Ceremonies

Mark the completion of your Teddy Bear Games with these special events.

Super Scrapbook

Capture fond memories of the Teddy Bear Games by making a class scrapbook. To make one, take photos of youngsters participating in the events. When the film has been developed, glue the photos to sheets of construction paper. Encourage youngsters to recall their memories of the events; then write their comments under and around the photos. Bind the pages between tagboard covers that have been cut slightly larger than the scrapbook pages. Place the finished scrapbook in your library center for youngsters to enjoy!

Marvelous Medals

What athletic event would be complete without the awarding of medals? Acknowledge the effort made by each student with a Teddy Bear Games Medal Of Participation. For each student and her teddy bear, duplicate copies of the medals on page 85 onto yellow construction paper. Cut the medals out; then glue each medal onto a blue construction-paper circle cut about one-quarter inch larger than the medal. Punch a hole in the top of each medal; then thread a length of yarn through the hole to create a necklace. Set the medals aside to present to students and their bears during your closing ceremonies (see "It's A Celebration!").

It's A Celebration!

Tantalize your little athletes' taste buds with some teddy-bear treats to celebrate their Teddy Bear Games accomplishments. Arrange your classroom tables into a circle. At each place setting, provide a peanut butter and honey sandwich cut into the shape of a bear (use a bear-shaped cookie cutter), some Teddy Grahams®, and a few Gummy bears. As youngsters are munching on their teddy treats, ask them to recap their favorite events; then present each athlete and his bear with medals of participation (see "Marvelous Medals") for a job well done!

Teddy-Bear Pattern
Use with "The Main Event" and "Bring In The Bears" on page 76, "Reading Marathon" on page 78, and "Teddy Estimates" on page 79.

Pass Card
Use with "Pass, Please" on page 77.

Pass Card for Teddy Bear Games

Opening Ceremonies	Reading Marathon	Bouncing Bears	Musical Bears
Edible Emblems	Teddy Estimates	Busy Bear Relay	Closing Ceremonies

Bear Invitation

Use with "Bring In The Bears" on page 76.

Dear _____,
(teddy bear name)

    I really need your help. The Teddy Bear Games are about to start at my school. All of the boys and girls are bringing their bears.

    We are going to have lots of fun playing games all week long. I can't do it without you.

    Please come to school with me tomorrow. We will have a great time playing all of the games, and you can stay at school until they are over. I can't wait. See you soon!

Love,

_____

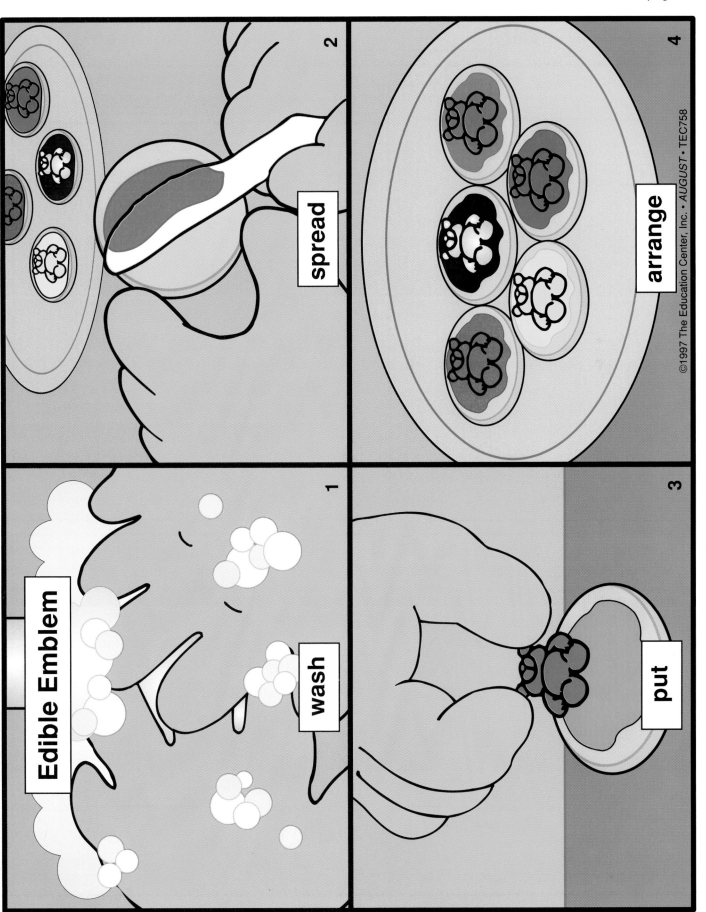

Teddy Bear Games Gazette

Date: _____

Today's Events:

Note To The Teacher: Use with "Teddy Bear Games Gazette" on page 77.

One Last Blast

Use the activities in this unit to punctuate summer's end with an explosion of learning and excitement! And be sure to take lots of photo memories along the way. Youngsters will have a blast!

ideas contributed by Linda Gordetsky and Mackie Rhodes

Wet And Wonderful

Start your end-of-summer celebration with the battery of wet activities described on these two pages. In advance send a copy of the parent letter on page 92 home with each child; then get set for a splash of a blast! Continue the fun with the less wet—but no less fun—ideas on pages 88–91.

A Splashy Tune

Teach youngsters this lively tune to sing as they splash in the sprinkler's spray.

One Last Blast For The Summer
(sung to the tune of "Take Me Out To The Ball Game")

One last blast for the summer.
One last blast before fall.
I'll run in the sun—
Feel the heat on my face.
Splish-splashing cool water
All over the place!

Now there's June, July, and yes,
　　August—
Each month is my summertime
　　friend.
For it's **one…two…three** months of
　　fun
Before summer's end!

Let's Limbo

Here's a new twist on an all-time favorite—dancing the limbo in dancing waters. To begin set up an oscillating sprinkler in an outdoor play area; then have a pair of volunteers stand in the path of the water spray while holding a wooden dowel horizontal to the ground. Play Greg and Steve's "Disco Limbo" on *We All Live Together, Volume 3* (Youngheart Records)—or another lively song—while swimsuited students dance the limbo under the dowel. After each dance round, ask the volunteers to lower the dowel; then challenge youngsters to once again perform their own version of a wet and wild limbo.

Balloons Overhead!

With each balloon burst in this outdoor activity will come a burst of laughter from your drenched students. In advance prepare a supply of water balloons; then have youngsters form a straight line, one behind another and an arm's length apart. Ask every other student in line to turn so that she faces one classmate and has her back to another. To play have students pass a water balloon overhead down the line. If the balloon bursts during a pass, the receiving child assumes the position at one end of the line; then the other students adjust their positions to reestablish the alternating line-up pattern. Play resumes with the new leader passing another water balloon down the line. Heads up!

Summer Science

Here's a question to ask during your last wet blast: Does the size of an object influence its ability to float in water? After youngsters discuss their responses to this question, divide the class into student pairs. Give each pair a copy of the recording form on page 92 and the items listed on that form. Ask one partner to place each listed item in a tub of water to test its buoyancy while the other partner marks the results on the recording form. After the partners complete their forms, invite each pair to share its results with the class. Does size make a difference?

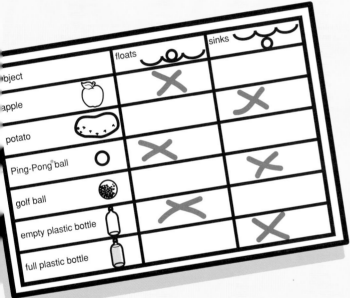

object	floats	sinks
apple	X	
potato		X
Ping-Pong ball	X	
golf ball		X
empty plastic bottle	X	
full plastic bottle		X

Water Paints

As part of your last blast and splash of the summer, involve youngsters in this freshening-up activity. To begin gather a collection of paintbrushes, rollers, and several water-filled paint trays, as well as a supply of painter's caps. Explain that after a long year, your school building and playground equipment could use a fresh paint job. Then invite each youngster to don a cap and assume the role of a painter. Provide each painter with the necessary tools and an area to paint; then encourage him to thoroughly cover his assigned area with a coat of water "paint." All fresh and ready for a new school year!

Amber

Bubble Babies

Compliments will bubble forth over these adorable creations. In advance mix the bubble recipe shown on this page. Then half-fill a plastic cup with the bubble solution. Stir in a few drops of food coloring. Have a child blow air into the cup using a straw; then remove the straw when the bubbles reach just above the rim of the cup. Help the child place a sheet of white paper over the top of the cup to capture a print of the bubble mound. Set the print—now a bubble-baby body—aside to dry; then have the youngster draw a head, arms, and legs on the body. Invite her to glue stretched cotton balls all around the bubble baby to achieve a cloudlike effect. Then display the pictures, with the edges slightly overlapping, to create a billowy sky full of bubble babies. It's a bubble-baby fantasy!

Bubble Mania

If your students are crazy about bubbles, here's a great way for them to blow off some of their late-summer energy. To begin mix up several batches of bubble solution following the recipe shown. Pour the mixture into a few shallow trays and widemouthed containers. While outdoors, give each child a container or tray of bubble solution; then engage her in a bubble-blowing frenzy using a variety of unusual bubble-blowing tools—such as plastic funnels, six-pack soda rings, cans with both ends removed, and plastic cups with holes poked through the bottoms. Also challenge her to catch bubbles using the same tool with which she blew them. Bubbles here. Bubbles there. Bubbles, bubbles, everywhere!

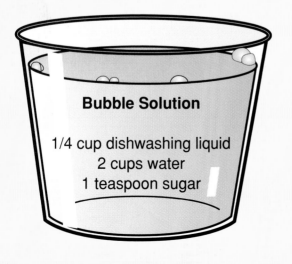

Bubble Solution

1/4 cup dishwashing liquid
2 cups water
1 teaspoon sugar

Chalk The Walk

Your young artists will delight in creating *and* erasing sidewalk masterpieces drawn with homemade chalk. To make sidewalk chalk, cover one end of each of several toilet-paper tubes with foil; then mix a small amount of powdered tempera paint with a quantity of Bondex® Plaster of Paris according to the package directions. Fill each tube with the mixture. Cover the open end of the tube with another piece of foil. Allow the mixture in the tubes to dry overnight; then peel each tube away from the hardened plaster. Invite youngsters to use the chalk to create artistic masterpieces on the school's canvas of sidewalks. Afterward have students erase their drawings with a spray or splash of water. Magnificent!

I Love Summer, "Yessirree"!

Use these student-made tambourines to tap into a categorizing game that will help students realize just how much fun summer holds. To begin give each youngster a small pie tin with prepunched holes around its rim and a plastic needle threaded with a one-foot length of yarn. Also provide a supply of loose jingle bells and small beads. Instruct each child to alternate stringing bells and beads onto his length of yarn as he sews the yarn through the pie-tin holes. Provide additional yarn lengths as necessary, helping him secure each length of yarn to the pie tin. To play have youngsters sit in a circle holding their tambourines. Call out an activity such as sledding, swimming, or camping. If a student thinks the named activity is appropriate for summer, have him shake his tambourine; then ask him to explain his reasoning. Afterward name the activity again. Invite all students who agree that it is a summertime activity to jump up, shake their tambourines, and recite the chant at left. Then repeat the game, naming a different activity. Summer is fun!

Summer. Summer.
One, two, three.
I love summer,
"Yessirree!"

Sun Sparklers

Reinforce the names of the summer months with this discus-toss game. To prepare label three separate boxes "June," "July," and "August." Duplicate several sun patterns (page 93) on tagboard; then cut out each pattern to serve as a template. To make a sun sparkler discus, use a permanent marker to trace the sun template on an inverted plastic plate. Decorate the resulting sun outline with glitter paint pens. After the paint dries, invite each youngster to practice tossing her sun sparkler into one of the labeled boxes; then ask her to name the month labeled on the box.

Melon Math

If you plan to include watermelon-eating in your summer's end activities, try this math idea using watermelon seeds. As each youngster eats her watermelon, ask her to put the seeds into a paper cup. Afterward have her wash and count her seeds, then tell the class the number of seeds that were in her slice of watermelon. Next, pair students and have them combine their seeds. Ask each pair to count the total number of seeds, then to evenly divide them between the two partners. Instruct one partner to create a design or pattern with her seeds; then challenge her partner to reproduce the watermelon-seed design or pattern. It's math the melon-seed way!

Sowing Summer Seeds

Spread your seed fun into youngsters' homes with these take-home watermelon planters. In advance duplicate the parent letter on page 94 for each student. To make a planter, use markers or tempera paints to decorate an inverted sturdy paper bowl to resemble a round slice of watermelon as shown. Cut the bowl in half; then glue the two bowl halves together to create a planter as shown. Add a thick line of glue along the inside seam of the planter to seal any gaps. After the glue dries, punch holes as shown; then thread a few lengths of yarn through the two holes on each side of the planter. Tie all the yarn ends together to create a hanger. Then send home with each child the parent letter, a small, zippered plastic bag of watermelon seeds (from "Melon Math"), a zippered bag full of potting soil, and his watermelon planter. After a few days, ask youngsters to tell the class about their family planting experiences; then periodically invite students to give progress reports on their watermelon plants. You'll be amazed at how quickly interest sprouts and grows on this topic!

Summertime Station

Toot! Toot! Invite youngsters aboard for a last blast around the tracks to review their special family summer activities. In advance send home a copy of the parent photo request on page 94 with each child. After students bring their photos to class, ask each child to decorate a construction-paper copy of the train pattern on page 95; then have him cut out his pattern. Instruct the student to glue his photo onto the cutout in the indicated space. Then invite each child, in turn, to don an engineer's cap and chug-a-chug his way before the class to tell about his pictured summer adventure. Write his dictation (in abbreviated terms, if necessary) on a construction-paper smoke puff; then display his train and smoke puff with the title "Summertime Station." Hop on board!

One lazy summer day...

Lazy, Crazy Days Of Summer

Roll out some blankets and towels for some lazy, crazy, end-of-summer fun. While lazing around outdoors on a summer day, engage youngsters in this build-a-story activity. Begin a story with "One lazy summer day…." Then invite one student at a time to add a line to the story, continuing until you give the signal, "Crazy summer day!" On that signal, the students will jump up and act out some crazy energy until you give the signal, "La-a-azy summer day." Then they will resume their relaxed positions on the blankets to begin a new story. After several rounds of storytelling, give each student a copy of the story page on page 96. Ask her to illustrate one of the class-created stories, then use her illustration to retell the story to the class.

Summer Favorites

If you've taken pictures of your one-last-blast activities, use this idea to help youngsters summarize their favorites. Ask each child to decorate a toilet-paper tube with brightly colored markers; then have her glue colorful strips of paper to both ends of the tube. After the glue dries, secretly slip a rolled picture of one of your class activities into each child's tube. Place all the tubes in a box; then invite each child in turn to pick a tube from the box. Ask her to remove the picture from the tube and show it to the class. Encourage each student to share a memory about the pictured activity, then to tell whether or not that particular activity was her favorite. Afterward have each child slip one of the pictures into her own tube to share with her family. (You might want to have extra pictures on hand to give every child a choice.) Such great summer memories!

Parent Letter
Use with "Wet And Wonderful" on page 86.

Dear Parent,
 Our class is planning some outdoor water fun as part of our "one last blast" to commemorate summer's end. To prepare your child for these activities, please send the following items on _____.

(date)

_____ swimsuit

_____ bath towel

_____ sunscreen

_____ sunglasses

_____ change of clothes

_____ large, resealable plastic bag (for wet clothes)

_____ flip-flops or water shoes (or any pair of shoes that can get wet)

Thank you!

Recording Form
Use with "Summer Science" on page 87.

Object	floats	sinks
apple		
potato		
Ping-Pong® ball		
golf ball		
empty plastic bottle		
full plastic bottle		

Parent Letter

Use with "Sowing Summer Seeds" on page 90.

Dear Parent,

Mmmm! We just enjoyed some tasty watermelon at school—and now we want to share some of that watermelon with you. Please help your child place the provided soil and seeds in the hanging planter; then together water and nurture the new sprouts. Take some time periodically to talk about and admire the growing vine with your child.

Thanks for supporting your child's learning.

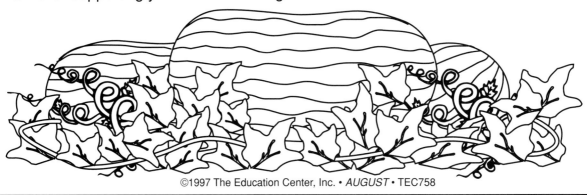

©1997 The Education Center, Inc. • *AUGUST* • TEC758

Parent Photo Request

Use with "Summertime Station" on page 91.

Dear Parent,

Our class is having a blast here at the end of the summer! As one of our activities, we will talk about a special summer activity in which each child's family has participated. Please send a photo of your child and/or family enjoying a trip, vacation, event, or other special activity from this summer. If desired write a brief description about the picture on the back. Your photo will be used in a display, then returned to you.

We appreciate your help and cooperation!

©1997 The Education Center, Inc. • *AUGUST* • TEC758

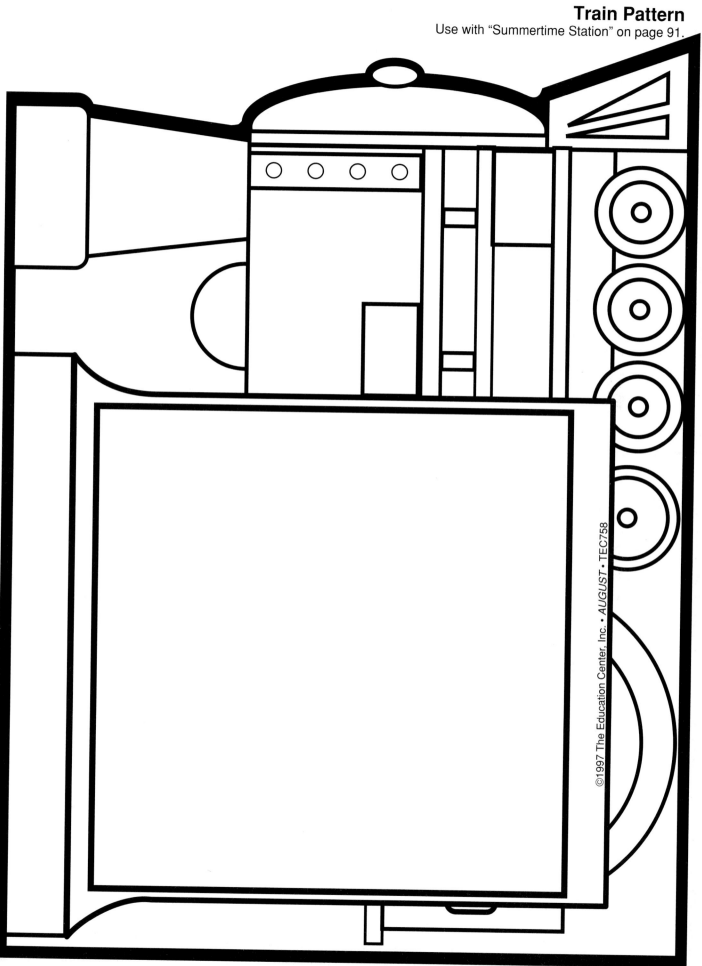

One lazy summer day...

Note To The Teacher: Use with "Lazy, Crazy Days Of Summer" on page 91.